P9-DBI-019

The Ultimate Reference Guide to the World's Most Popular Martial Art

TAE KWON DO

Yeon Hee Park
Yeon Hwan Park
Jon Gerrard

Updated Edition

무술의 최고 참고서

세계에서 가장 인기있는

Checkmark Books™
An imprint of Facts On File, Inc.

796.815
PAR

TAE KWON DO:
The Ultimate Reference Guide to the World's Most Popular Martial Art,
Updated Edition

Copyright © 1989, 1999 by Facts On File, Inc.
First edition 1989
Updated edition 1999

All rights reserved. No part of this book may be reproduced or utilized in any
form or by any means, electronic or mechanical, including photocopying, record-
ing, or by any information storage or retrieval systems, without permission in
writing from the publisher. For information contact:

Checkmark Books
An imprint of Facts On File, Inc.
11 Penn Plaza
New York NY 10001

Library of Congress Cataloging-in-Publication Data

Park, Yeon Hee.
    Tae kwon do: the ultimate reference guide to the world's most
popular martial art / Yeon Hee Park, Yeon Hwan Park, and Jon
Gerrard. — Updated ed.
        p. cm.
    Includes bibliographical references and index.
    ISBN-0-8160-3838-4. — ISBN 0-8160-3839-2 (pbk.)
    1. Tae kwon do. I. Park, Yeon Hwan. II. Gerrard, Jon.
    III. Title.
    GV1114.9.P35   1999
    796.815'3—dc21   98–34013

Checkmark Books are available at special discounts when purchased in bulk quantities
for businesses, associations, institutions, or sales promotions. Please call our Special
Sales Department in New York at 212/967-8800 or 800/322-8755.

You can find Facts On File on the World Wide Web at http://www.factsonfile.com

Cover and interior text designed by Ron Monteleone

Printed in the United States of America

RRD FOF 10 9 8 7 6 5 4 3 2

CONTENTS

PREFACE

We have often been asked to define what Tae Kwon Do is, to encapsulate in a few words that which for many is a vague and elusive concept. When answering such a question, the first thing we try to impress upon the person is that Tae Kwon Do is not just self-defense training or punching and kicking. The art is far more than simple physical conditioning, mental training and philosophical study. It has to do with the development of the Tae Kwon Do spirit, which carries over into all aspects of a student's life. And when we refer to students of the art, we include all teachers of the art as well, for we too are always growing and learning through Tae Kwon Do. This concept of the spirit of Tae Kwon Do is where the elusive answer to our question is found, for this is in essence the definition of Tae Kwon Do.

In English, the literal translation of Tae Kwon Do is "the art of kicking and punching." *Tae* means "to kick," *Kwon* means "to punch" and *Do* means "art." But this is only a superficial translation. *Do* in Korean implies a philosophical viewpoint or way of approaching life—a means by which enlightenment is achieved. This is the ultimate aim of Tae Kwon Do. Through rigorous physical training students of the art seek to improve themselves, physically, mentally and spiritually. On the pages of this book you will see only the physical techniques explained and demonstrated. Yet this is simply the veneer of our art, the only part of our art that can be captured and demonstrated by words and pictures. That which is truly the essence of Tae Kwon Do cannot be seen, touched, smelled, tasted or heard. It can only be experienced.

You may have noticed that we still have not yet answered the question of what Tae Kwon Do is. Our answer is to invite the questioner to experience Tae Kwon Do by studying with us. We now extend that same invitation to you. Come, study and experience with us.

Master Yeon Hee Park
Master Yeon Hwan Park
Jon Gerrard

ACKNOWLEDGMENTS

We would like to thank the following people for sacrificing their own time to help us with this book:

Louis (Louie) Arcila
John R. Buran
Daniel (Danny) Cordova
Norman Dion
Mitchell L. Drucker
Nancy Hendler
Thomas Honohan
Mitchell Kosheff
Frank Lagumina
Kirk Larsen
Pauljames (Paul) Lazo
Sal Menniti
Margaret (Peggy) McCormick
Antonio (Tony) Rambla
Michael (Mike) Semer
Louis Shahin
Dawn Smallwood
Robert (Bobby) Strangio
Professor Howard Wasserman
Kathleen (Kathy) Westerberg
F. Dana Winslow, Esq.

THE WORLD TAEKWONDO FEDERATION

Recognized by the International Olympic Committee
Affiliated with the General Association of International Sports Federations.

635 YUKSAMDONG, KANGNAMKU
SEOUL KOREA (135)
CABLE ADDRESS : WORLD TAEKWONDO

TELEPHONE : 82.2.566-2505
          82.2.557-5446
TELEX   : K28870 WTFED
FACSIMILE : 82.2.553-4728

WTF PRESIDENT'S REMARKS ON
TAE KWON DO

I am pleased to endorse this book on the art of Taekwondo. The Park brothers are well known throughout the Taekwondo community for both their excellent skill as competitors and their diligence as instructors. They are among those most dedicated to the propagation and development of Taekwondo in the United States.

I was glad, therefore, when I learned of their plan to write this book. The Parks have done an extraordinary job in putting this complicated book together. I consider TAE KWON DO to be the most comprehensive work on the subject, and I believe it will be widely used by practitioners of the art. What the authors have done is to create the perfect student's guidebook on the art of Taekwondo. Every aspect of our art is clearly illustrated and explained, enabling students to practice with great ease on their own. While not intended to serve as a replacement for live instruction, the book is nonetheless an invaluable learning aid.

I confidently endorse their book.

Un Yong Kim
President

INTRODUCTION

THE HISTORY OF AN ART

A s it is literally translated from the Korean, *Tae* means "to kick" or "to strike with the foot," *Kwon* means "fist" or "to strike with the hand," and *Do* means "discipline" or "art." Taken together, Tae Kwon Do means "the art of kicking and punching"—"the art of unarmed combat." Modern-day Tae Kwon Do, as it has come to be developed over the years, is a unique martial art incorporating both the quick, straight-line movements that characterize the various Japanese systems and the flowing circular movements of most Chinese styles. But more than this, what truly distinguishes Tae Kwon Do are its varied and uniquely powerful kicking techniques. It is this prominent use of leg and kicking techniques that sets Tae Kwon Do apart from all other martial arts systems. Yet, Tae Kwon Do is far more than simply a system concerned with physical prowess, for it is also an art directed toward the moral development of its students.

The earliest records of Tae Kwon Do practice date back to about 50 B.C. During this time, Korea was divided into three kingdoms: Silla, which was founded on the Kyongju plain in 57 B.C.; Koguryo, founded in the Yalu River Valley in 37 B.C.; and Baekche, founded in the southwestern area of the Korean peninsula in 18 B.C.. Evidence of the practice of *Taek Kyon* (the earliest known form of Tae Kwon Do) has been found in paintings on the ceiling of the Muyong-chong, a royal tomb from the Koguryo dynasty. These and other mural paintings show unarmed combatants using techniques that are virtually identical to those of modern-day Tae Kwon Do. Of particular interest are details that show the use of the knife hand, fist and classical fighting stances, all components of modern Tae Kwon Do.

Although Tae Kwon Do first appeared in the Koguryo kingdom, it is Silla's warrior nobility, the Hwarang, who are credited with the growth and spread of the art throughout Korea. Of the three kingdoms, Silla was the first to be formed, but it remained the smallest and least civilized. Its coastline was constantly under attack by Japanese pirates. After Silla appealed for help against the continual harassment by the Japanese pirates, King Gwanggaeto, the 19th in the line of Koguryo monarchs, sent a force of 50,000 soldiers into neighboring Silla to help the smaller kingdom drive out the pirates. It is at this time that Taek Kyon is thought to have been introduced to Silla's warrior class, handed down in strict secrecy to a few select Sillan warriors by early masters of the art.

These Taek Kyon-trained warriors became known as the Hwarang. Founded initially as a military academy for the young nobility of Silla, the society of the Hwarang-do ("the way of flowering manhood") adopted Taek Kyon as a part of its basic training regimen. The society was an elite group, consisting of the Hwarang, or leaders, who were selected from among the sons of royalty between the ages of 16 and 20, and the Nangdo, or cadets, who were assembled from the rest of the young nobility and who totaled between 200 and 1000 at any given time. The young men within the society were educated in many disciplines, including history, Confucian philosophy, ethics, Buddhist morality, riding, archery, sword play, military tactics and, of course, Taek Kyon. The guiding principles of the Hwarang-do education were based on the Five Codes of Human Conduct, as established by the Buddhist scholar Wonkang. These axioms are:

> Be loyal to your country
> Be obedient to your parents
> Be trustworthy to your friends
> Never retreat in battle
> Never make an unjust kill

Taek Kyon was taught in conjunction with the Five Codes of Human Conduct so that it became a way of life for the young men, a code of moral behavior that served to guide their lives and the use to which they put their training in Taek Kyon.

Today, these codes are reflected in the so-called 11 commandments of modern Tae Kwon Do. As with the original codes of conduct, these modern axioms are used to guide the moral development of students of the art, and no student who does not fully understand these tenets can ever hope to master the true essence of the art.

> Loyalty to your country
> Respect your parents
> Faithfulness to your spouse
> Respect your brothers and sisters
> Loyalty to your friends
> Respect your elders
> Respect your teachers
> Never take life unjustly

Indomitable spirit
Loyalty to your school
Finish what you begin

Along with their training in fundamental education and military skills, the Hwarang were also skilled in poetry, singing and dancing, and were encouraged to travel throughout the peninsula in order to learn about the regions and people. These traveling warriors were responsible for the spread of Taek Kyon throughout Korea during the Silla dynasty, which lasted from A.D. 668 to A.D. 935. During this era, Taek Kyon remained primarily a sports and recreational activity designed to improve physical fitness (although it was nonetheless quite a formidable system of self-defense). It was not until the Koryo dynasty, which began in 935 and lasted until 1392, that the focus of the art was changed. During this time, Taek Kyon became known as Subak, and during the reign of King Uijong (between the years of 1147 and 1170) it changed from a system designed primarily to promote fitness into a fighting art.

The first book widely available on the art was written during the Yi dynasty (1397 to 1907) to promote the art among the population in general. Prior to this, the art had been restricted primarily to the military nobility. The publication of this book and the subsequent popularizing of the art among the general public were responsible for the survival of Subak during this era, for during the second half of the Yi dynasty, political conflict and the de-emphasis of military activities in favor of more scholarly pursuits led to a significant reduction in the practice of the art. Records of the practice of Subak are sparse during this time. The art again returned to its former role as a recreational and fitness activity, with the exception that now it was the general population which maintained the art and not the nobility. Subak as an art became fragmented and diffused throughout the country, and its practice continued to decline until only incomplete remnants remained. What limited knowledge there was of the art was handed down from one generation to the next within individual families that generally practiced it in secret.

It was not until 1909 that Korea's fighting arts experienced a marked resurgence, for in that year the Japanese invaded Korea, occupying the country for the next 36 years. During this time, the Japanese resident general officially banned the practice of all military arts for native Koreans. Ironically, this very act sparked a renewed growth of Subak. Patriots, fueled by a hatred of their subjugators, organized themselves into underground factions and traveled to remote Buddhist temples to study the martial arts. Still others left Korea to work and study in China and even Japan itself, where they were exposed to the fighting arts native to those countries. In Korea, Subak/Taek Kyon was kept alive through the efforts of a number of famous masters of the Korean fighting arts. Eventually, the underground nature of the martial arts in Korea changed when, in 1943, first Judo and then Karate and Kung-fu were officially introduced. The following two years saw a dramatic increase in interest in the martial arts throughout the country. But it was not until Korea's liberation in 1945 that its own fighting arts finally took root and began to flourish. For many years, a variety of Korean martial art styles existed throughout the country. These styles varied from one another according to the amount of influence each master had absorbed from the numerous Chinese and Japanese styles and the extent to which the native Subak/ Taek Kyon had been modified over the years.

The first *kwan* ("school") to teach a native Korean style of martial art was opened in 1945 in Yong Chun, Seoul. This *dojang* (gymnasium) was named the Chung Do Kwan. Later that same year, the Moo Duk Kwan and the Yun Moo Kwan also opened in Seoul. The following year, the Chang Moo Kwan followed by the Chi Do Kwan were founded. Seven other major schools were formed between 1953 and the early 1960s, the three most prominent being the Ji Do Kwan, the Song Moo Kwan and the Oh Do Kwan, all of which were opened between 1953 and 1954. Although each of these schools claimed to teach the traditional Korean martial art, each one emphasized a different aspect of Tae Kyon/Subak and various names emerged for each system. Styles became known as Soo Bahk Do, Kwon Bop, Kong Soo Do, Tae Soo Do and Dang Soo Do. There were also those who claimed to teach traditional Taek Kyon.

Dissension between the various *kwans* prevented the formation of a central regulating board for 10 years. Yet, during those years, the martial arts gained a strong foothold within the newly formed Korean Armed Forces (1945), with Taek Kyon becoming a regular part of military training. In early 1946, masters of the art began teaching Taek Kyon to troops stationed in Kwang Ju. This set the foundation for the great turning point in the Korean martial arts in 1952. That year, at the height of the Korean War, President Syngman Rhee watched a half-hour demonstration by Korean martial arts masters. Rhee was so impressed with what he saw that he ordered training in the martial arts to be adopted as part of regular military training. This single act was to have a far reaching effect on the Korean martial arts. Later that same year, a master was sent to Fort Benning, Georgia for special training in radio communications. The master had been one of those to perform before President Rhee, and Rhee had taken special notice of his abilities prior to his assignment to the United States. During his stay in Georgia, the master demonstrated his art to both the military and the general public, further publicizing Korea's fighting art. In Korea, special commando groups of martial arts-trained soldiers were formed to fight against the communist forces of North Korea. The most famous of these special forces was known as the Black Tigers, who staged many espionage missions across the borders in hostile territory. Occasionally they performed assassinations. Many great martial artists lost their lives during this time, including the founders of the Chang Moo Kwan and the Yun Moo Kwan.

Following the end of the war in 1953, the Korean 29th Infantry Division was established on Che Ju island. This unit was responsible for all Taek Kyon training in the Korean Army. Two years later, on April 11, 1955, a meeting was convened to unify the various *kwans* under a common name. The name of Tae Soo Do was accepted by the majority of the *kwan* masters, who then agreed to merge their various styles for the mutual benefit of all schools. However, two years later the name was once again changed, this time to the familiar Tae Kwon Do. Chosen both because it accurately describes the nature of the art (comprised of both hand and foot techniques) as well as for its similarity to the art's early name of Taek Kyon, Tae Kwon Do has been the recognized name for the Korean martial arts since that day. However, although most of the *kwans* merged under this common name, there were a few who did not. It has never been clear which of the original eight did in fact merge in 1955, but of those who did not, only Hapkido remains as a recognized separate art in itself. Yet, despite the historic merging, dissension between the *kwans* did not end at that meeting in 1955. Until the formation of the Korean Tae Kwon Do Association on September 14, 1961, and indeed for a few years thereafter, there remained much animosity between the various masters.

The first leaders of the Korean Tae Kwon Do Association saw the potential for the spread and growth of their art and used their authority to send instructors and demonstration teams all over the world, spreading the art to every continent. In Korea, the study of Tae Kwon Do spread rapidly from the army into high schools and colleges. *Dojangs* for the general public sprang up everywhere. Tae Kwon Do had begun to blossom. Within a very brief time, the art had developed such a reputation for being an effective fighting system that during the Vietnam War, the South Vietnamese government requested instructors to train its troops. During the 1960s, thousands of Tae Kwon Do demonstrators performed around the world before fascinated governments, which with few exceptions followed up such exhibitions with calls for Korean instructors to teach in their countries. By the beginning of the 1970s, Tae Kwon Do had firmly established itself worldwide.

On May 28, 1973 a new, worldwide organization, the World Tae Kwon Do Federation (WTF), was formed. Since that day, all Tae Kwon Do activities outside of Korea have been coordinated by the WTF, the only official organization recognized by the Korean government as an international regulating body for Tae Kwon Do. Also in May 1973, the first biennial World Tae Kwon Do Championships were held in Seoul as a prelude to the inauguration of the WTF. Since then, the world championships have been held in many countries around the world, including the United States, West Germany, South America and Denmark.

It was Tae Kwon Do's prominence in the circle of international sports which brought the art to the attention of the General Association of International Sports Federation (GAISF). GAISF is an association of all international sports, both Olympic and non-Olympic, with direct ties to the International Olympic Committee (IOC). Under the auspices of GAISF, Tai Kwon Do as a sport was introduced to the IOC, which recognized and admitted the WTF in July 1980. Not long after this initial contact, Tae Kwon Do as a sport was given a tremendous honor. At the General Session of the IOC in May of 1982, Tae Kwon Do was designated an official Demonstration Sport for the 1988 Olympic Games in Seoul, Korea. There, under the inspirational leadership of their coach, Grandmaster Yeon Hwan Park, the United States women's team secured the first-place trophy. The U.S. men's team finished a respectable second, topped only by the Korean national team.

This exposure at the 24th Olympic Games brought the art to the attention of the general public for the first time. Audiences whose knowledge of the martial arts had been restricted to Japanese Karate-do and Chinese Kung Fu were now afforded a look at the Korean martial art. Although having aspects similar to both Karate-do and Kung Fu, Tae Kwon Do has an element that sets it apart from all other systems. For sporting contests, competitors are outfitted with padding that protects them from serious injury while imposing very little restriction on movement. As a result, audiences witnessed martial art competitors landing full-power techniques that could otherwise cripple or kill. And the techniques they saw were predominated by high, quick kicking and dynamic spinning. Tae Kwon Do had blossomed.

As a testament to its popularity, the art was once again selected to appear as a Demonstration Sport at the 1992 Olympics in Barcelona, Spain. Once again the audience response to Tae Kwon Do was overwhelming. As a result of its obvious popularity, Tae Kwon Do was accorded its crowning achievement in September of 1994 when it was accepted as a full medal sport for the 2000 Olympic Games in Sydney, Australia.

In the short time since the WTF was established in 1973, Tae Kwon Do has grown with unprecedented rapidity as a worldwide sport. Today, with more than 30 million practitioners in 163 countries, Tae Kwon Do has earned the distinction of being recognized as the most widely practiced martial art system in the world.

1
WARMING
UP EXERCISES

GETTING YOUR BODY READY

Any experienced athlete knows the value of preparing the body before engaging in physical activity. This is of course true for the practice of Tae Kwon Do, and given the nature of the art, it is especially important for students to prepare their bodies before practice. Tae Kwon Do requires much from a student physically: the entire cardiovascular system is involved; muscles and joints work quickly and repeatedly as the hands and feet snap out powerfully to strike and kick. If the body has not been properly prepared for this type of activity, cramping can develop in the muscles or, more seriously, injury can occur to the joints, ligaments and tendons. This is not to say that the practice of this art is limited only to those individuals who are in the best of physical condition. Many students first begin their study of Tae Kwon Do at an advanced age and yet are still able to develop into powerful martial artists. What is important to remember is that even masters of the art stretch and warm up their bodies before practice to prevent injury.

On the following pages we have compiled a comprehensive set of exercises that limber and strengthen every major muscle and joint group of the body. We strongly recommend you do all the exercises prior to attempting any of the techniques of the art. By the time all of the exercises have been performed, the body should be completely flexible and practice can begin without fear of injury. It's important to work on limbering the pelvic area and legs, as these areas of the body need to be particularly flexible to deliver the variety of powerful kicking techniques that characterize Tae Kwon Do.

Caution should be observed when you first try any of the following exercises. In general, stretches should be done only to the point where you first feel discomfort, but before you feel any real pain. Do the stretches as directed, moving slowly and *without* bouncing, which will strain tendons and may result in injury. Although there is no set number of times a specific exercise should be repeated, on the average eight to 10 repetitions of each exercise will prepare your body sufficiently to begin practice. Remember that if you take a break in your training and your body has cooled down, it may be necessary to go through the stretches again.

ONE-PERSON EXERCISES

A   B   C   D

Hurdler's Stretch: Position yourself as illustrated (A), being careful to keep the knee of the front leg straight and the toes of that foot pulled back throughout the stretch. Begin by bending at the waist to place your chest to the thigh of the lead leg and hold for a count of two (B). Next, turn and bend forward to place your chest to the floor between your knees (C). Finally, twist far to the side and put your head to the back knee and hold for a count of two (D). Repeat. Do not forget to switch legs and do both sides. This exercise loosens the hip joints and stretches the muscles of the groin and the front and rear thighs.

A   B

Front Split: While keeping the knees straight, lower yourself into a front split as far as you can and hold the stretch (A). After holding the stretch for a while, lower your chest to the front leg (B). This exercise loosens the hip joints and stretches the muscles of the groin and front and rear thighs.

A   B

Lotus Knee Press: Sit on the floor with your legs bent and the soles of your feet together. Be sure to pull the heels into the groin as much as possible and use your elbows to press your knees down toward the floor (A). Then, while still holding ankles, bend to bring your chest to your feet (B). This exercise loosens the hip joints and stretches the groin muscles.

A   B   C

Side Split: While keeping the knees straight, spread your feet apart and lower yourself into a side split (A). (If you are not stretched enough to lower completely into a side split, be sure to support your weight with your hands until the muscles stretch to prevent tendon strain). After holding the stretch for a while, lower your chest to each knee (B), then the floor (C). This exercise loosens the hip joints and stretches the groin and backs of the thighs.

Back Arch: Lay on the floor as shown in (A) with feet flat on the floor and hands on either side of the head. Push up and arch your body toward the ceiling and hold (B). Repeat. This exercise loosens the spine and stretches the chest and abdominal muscles.

Body Rock: Lay with chest on floor and grasp ankles. Arch your back and pull your ankles up as shown here. This exercise stretches and strengthens the stomach and lower back muscles.

Body Tuck: Raise yourself into a shoulder stand (A). While holding this position, spread legs as far apart as possible (B), then bring them back together and spread them apart again in a steady rhythm. Next, bring feet together into the starting position and alternately kick the legs front and back, again with a steady rhythm (C). Lastly, bring your feet together once more and bend at the waist until toes touch the floor with knees straight (D). This exercise loosens the hips and stretches the groin, rear thigh and lower back muscles.

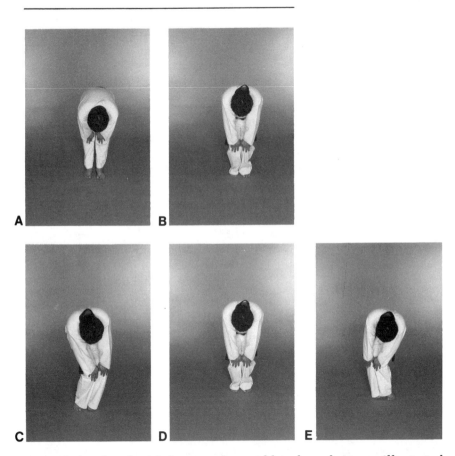

Knee Twist: Stand with feet together and hands on knees as illustrated (A). Rotate knees clockwise (B,C) and counterclockwise (D,E) slowly raising heels from the floor. This exercise loosens the ankle and knee joints.

Knee Bends: Stand with feet together and hands on knees as illustrated (A). Lower hips until knees are fully flexed and bounce lightly for a count of two (B). Straighten legs and press back *lightly* on knees for a count of two (C). Repeat. It is important to remember throughout this exercise that you must help to support your weight with your hands to prevent knee tendon strain. Your knees are the most important areas of your legs in delivering kicks effectively. The knee is also the most delicate and vulnerable part of your leg. *Never do deep knee bends without helping to support your weight in this way or serious damage could result.* This exercise loosens the knee joints.

Front and Back Side Split: While standing as in (A), bend and stretch to touch the floor in front of you for a count two (B). Then reach between your legs as far to the back as possible for a count of two (C). Then straighten and arch back, pushing your pelvis forward for a count of two (D). This exercise loosens the hip joints and stretches the muscles of the groin.

Leg Stretch: Support your entire body weight on one foot as you straighten the other leg out to one side. Bend the knee of the supporting leg and lower pelvis toward the floor while flexing the foot of the nonsupporting leg and pulling the toes back (A). Continue to lower pelvis to the floor as far as possible (B). This exercise stretches the muscles in the back of the leg and is an essential exercise for high kicking.

Windmills: Stand with your feet spread approximately twice your shoulder width (A), bend and twist to reach the right hand to the left foot (B), then twist in the other direction and reach the left hand to the right foot (C). The exercise should be done with a regular rhythm. This exercise loosens the hip joints and waist and stretches the muscles of the groin.

Trunk Twist: Stand upright with feet approximately shoulder width apart as shown here (A). Rotate the pelvis clockwise (B,C,D,E) and then counterclockwise. This exercise loosens the waist.

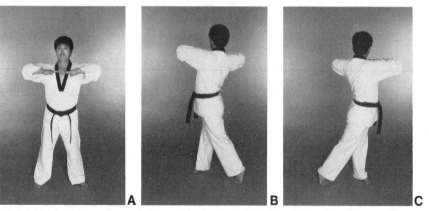

Waist Twist: Stand upright with feet approximately shoulder width apart and raise your arms from your sides (A). Twist first to the right (B)

and then to the left (C) as far as possible without raising your heels from the floor. Do the exercise with a regular rhythm. This exercise loosens the waist.

Side Stretch: Stand with feet spread approximately two shoulder widths apart (A). Raise your right arm over your head, lean as far to the left as possible and hold for two to three seconds (B). Straighten and repeat to the right (C). This exercise loosens the waist and stretches the muscles on the sides of the body under the arms.

Chest Stretch: Stand with feet shoulder width apart and bend slightly forward at the waist with arms hanging limply (A). Arch backward and look up as arms are brought above the head and spread apart (B). Then relax and bend forward while allowing arms to swing down and back (C). Repeat. This exercise stretches the muscles of the chest.

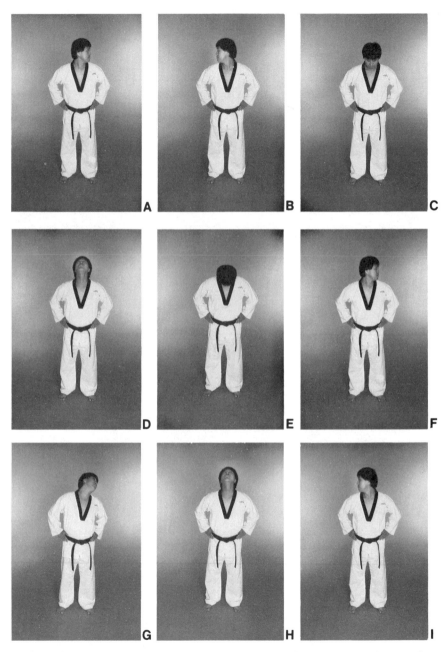

Neck Roll: While standing upright, twist head slowly from side to side (A,B) and front to back (C,D). Next, let head fall forward and rotate slowly in a circle, clockwise and counterclockwise (E,F,G,H,I). This exercise loosens the neck.

TWO-PERSON EXERCISES

A   B   C   D

Two-Person Side Split: Face your partner as pictured here (A). Spread your legs apart as far as possible so that your partner can place the soles of his feet against your inner ankles and press the legs farther apart. After holding this stretch for a while, turn and bend at the waist to place the chest on each thigh (B)(C). Finally, bend forward and have your partner place his hands on your shoulders so that he can pull you forward and press you down to the floor (D). This exercise loosens the hip joints and stretches the groin, the backs of the thighs and the lower back muscles.

A   B

C   D   E

Body Fold: Sit back to back with your partner as shown in (A). While keeping the knees straight, your partner will press backward (B) until your chest rests on your thighs (C). After holding this stretch for a while, return to an upright position, spread feet apart into a side split (D) and have your partner press you down again (E). This exercise stretches and loosens the groin and the backs of the legs.

Leg Raise: Stand facing your partner and have him grasp the ankle of one leg and lift it to his shoulder as pictured here. This exercise helps to loosen the hip joint and stretch the rear thigh muscles.

Back Stretch: Stand back to back with your partner as illustrated in (A), with your hands above your head. Have your partner grasp your wrists and then lift you onto his back (B) as he bends forward, stretching the spine and loosening the shoulders and chest (C).

Sit-ups: Although this is not a stretching exercise, we have included sit-ups here because of the tremendous importance associated with strong abdominal muscles. Unlike the back, which is supported by the spine, the abdomen has no bone structure to support it and must rely instead on the strength of the stomach muscles alone. Further, strong stomach muscles assist in the ability of the student to kick powerfully—something very necessary in Tae Kwon Do. Note that the students pictured here twist when up, reaching to one knee with the opposite elbow, in order to insure that the full range of abdominal muscles are strengthened.

2
BASIC TECHNIQUES

All techniques of Tae Kwon Do fall into one of four general categories: stances, blocks, strikes and kicks. The approach of Tae Kwon Do is direct and uncomplicated, its very strength derived from its seeming simplicity. Unlike other systems, such as certain styles of Kung-fu, where complex maneuvers are learned to deal with specific defensive situations, Tae Kwon Do encourages spontaneous reaction by its students. The techniques themselves are geared for practical efficiency, with the blocking techniques developed to protect specific areas of the body (although not necessarily against specified forms of attack) and the striking and kicking techniques to direct maximum force in a variety of directions. Thus a trained student of Tae Kwon Do, when confronted with an attack to the head, for example, possesses a wide array of defenses and counterattacks that can be employed effectively. The techniques of some other martial arts systems provide elaborate, esoteric means of dealing with particular types of attack. The problem with this approach is that if the defender misreads the attack, or if the attacker is unorthodox, the defense may prove to be ineffective. Tae Kwon Do avoids this problem by developing sound, general techniques, and it leaves the specific application of those techniques to the trained intuition of the individual student in real-life situations. In this way, students of this art are prepared for a virtually infinite variety of attacks.

Tae Kwon Do is often compared (and confused with) a number of other systems, most usually Japanese Karate-do. At one time, when the art was first introduced into the United States, Tae Kwon Do was popularly known in the West as Korean Karate. While there are some superficial similarities between these two systems, each martial art is a distinct system emphasizing different things. Specifically, Tae Kwon Do can be differentiated from other systems by its emphasis on kicking techniques and a mobile and upright fighting stance. Consider the anatomical structure of the human leg in comparison to that of the arm. A leg can reach almost twice as far as an arm, delivering a blow from a much greater distance. And the heavy musculature of the leg makes it many times as powerful as an arm. Thus, a properly executed kick can deliver far more power than it is possible to generate with an arm, while at the same time keeping your opponent at a safe distance. Those who have any knowledge of the martial arts are aware that virtually every system employs kicking techniques, many of which are similar to those of Tae Kwon Do. The important difference between these others and Tae Kwon Do, however, is *the manner in which kicks are delivered.*

Tae Kwon Do emphasizes the quick retraction of the striking limb (arm and leg) following the delivery of an attack, as opposed to Japanese Karate-do, for example, in which the limb remains more rigidly extended for a brief time following the blow. The advantage of the rapid retraction of the limb is that it enables the student of Tae Kwon Do to deliver multiple strikes with great speed. Further, blows from rigidly extended limbs are much easier to evade in a real-life situation, whereas quickly retracted blows snap out with such speed that an opponent is hard pressed to block or evade them. There are those, however, who argue that such rapidly retracted, or "snap" techniques cannot deliver the same power as the more rigid techniques. We believe this is a misconception. When a student of Tae Kwon Do learns the proper use of his or her pelvis in the delivery of a technique, the same level of power can be generated as with a Karate kick, and without the rigidity and exposed vulnerability inherent in other approaches. Another danger with the more rigidly extended limb: The longer the limb remains extended away from the body, the more opportunity an opponent has to grab and manipulate that limb. The "snap" techniques of Tae Kwon Do make this virtually impossible as well.

As we mentioned above, Tae Kwon Do is characterized by its unique array of kicking techniques. The strength and reach of the leg make it an ideal tool for unarmed defense. The power generated by these techniques, however, comes from the proper use of body mechanics that Tae Kwon Do has developed over the centuries. But in order for any technique to be optimally effective, the defender must adopt a properly aligned stance that can support and help transmit power into the technique. This then brings us to the fourth and final general category of techniques: stances. Although the most basic of all techniques, we cannot overemphasize the importance of developing proper stances. If a student works very hard to perfect his punching and kicking techniques but cannot support those techniques with a proper stance, he will never be able to generate power. The key to generating power is learning to use the hips and waist properly. This is something that only comes with time and practice—there is no shortcut. If you apply yourself dilligently, though, you will soon reach the point where you will come to "feel" when your stance is proper. Then you will be on the road to developing power.

On the following pages, we have separated the basic techniques of Tae Kwon Do into the four general categories: stances, blocks, strikes and kicks. While the techniques presented are not an exhaustive list of every Tae Kwon Do technique, these are the basic techniques that students of the art must master in order to achieve the level of first-degree black belt. We have illustrated each of the blocking, striking and kicking techniques from a single stance (usually a kicking stance) and from a single camera angle. Furthermore, we have not illustrated all of the various possible applications of each technique. Our focus in this chapter is on providing the reader with a working understanding of the basic techniques and illustrating the proper form used when a technique is done correctly. Variations in applications of techniques will be discussed in Chapter 4, which deals in depth with sparring techniques.

STANCES

Before we illustrate specific stances, we want to discuss the proper way in which to hold your hands. Proper hand positioning not only protects the body adequately but also facilitates quicker movement and aids in the generation of power. The proper hand position is called the guard position.

A   **B**

Guard Position: Illustrations (A) and (B) (front and side views) show the proper guard position you should adopt in any defensive situation. As it is shown here, the leading hand is held in front of the body between chin level and the leading shoulder, while the rear hand is held just below shoulder level in front of the chest. This position allows quick hand motion in all directions while providing good protection at the same time.

A   B

Attention Stance: The attention stance is a formal (i.e., noncombat) stance which expresses respect for another as well as personal discipline. When you hold an attention stance you focus all of your attention on one thing—your instructor when he is speaking, or your opponent before the start of a match. It is this unwavering focus of attention that shows your own personal discipline and your respect for another. Very simply, the attention stance is a rigid stance with the feet together and the hands held flat against the thighs (A). The attention stance is also the position adopted before bowing to a fellow student or an opponent before a match (B). Note that the eyes are focused down at the floor during the bow so as not to insult the person being bowed to. This is an important but often overlooked detail of etiquette during a bow. To keep your eyes on an opponent during a bow indicates that you do not trust him.

Ready Stance: While standing in an upright posture with feet spread shoulder width apart and weight placed evenly on both feet, bring both fists up before your face (A), then slowly (over a period of three seconds) lower them to the level of your belt (B), to finally (after pausing for one second in this position) snap both hands out powerfully to a distance of about two fists from the front of your belt with the thumbs no more than two inches apart (C). This stance is used by students to prepare themselves for activity. While maintaining this stance, a student's gaze is focused directly ahead with his thoughts concentrated on the action he is about to perform. This stance precedes all of the forms (*poomse*) of the art.

Horseback Riding Stance: Stand with feet spread apart to double shoulder width and bend knees to lower the pelvis. Raise both arms to the front (A), and quickly draw the hands back into chambered position at the belt (B). The body must remain in an erect posture with the knees pressed outward, *not* bent inward, and the buttocks on the same line as the heels. The toes point directly forward and both feet should rest flat on the floor. Weight is evenly placed on both feet. This stance is very strong from side to side for either attack or defense.

Forward Stance: Step forward with one foot to a distance of two shoulder widths. The rear knee is locked straight while the front leg is bent so that the shin is perpendicular to the floor. The rear foot is turned to point as directly forward as possible without the heel raising off the floor. Weight is distributed with 60 percent on the forward leg and 40 percent on the rear leg. The feet must not be any narrower (side to side) than shoulder width to insure stability. The body is held properly erect and the hips are turned square to the forward direction. The correct positioning of the hips is essential in the forward stance to gain maximum power and stability. If the hips are turned at all, the stance loses its effectiveness. This stance is very strong for either attacking or defending from the front.

Back Stance: Turn the foot of the rear leg outward until it is perpendicular to the forward direction, then step forward with the leading leg a distance of one and one-half shoulder widths. Bend both knees, making sure to keep them pressed outward. Weight is distributed with 60 percent supported by the rear leg and 40 percent on the lead leg. Note that the heel of the rear leg is on the same line as the front foot. The body is maintained in an erect position and is turned so that the chest points 45 degrees from the forward direction. This stance combines the front to back and side to side strength of both the horseback riding and forward stances, plus allows for more mobility than either of the others. And with the body turned at an angle to the forward direction, the defender presents a smaller target to the opponent, making this a particularly effective combat stance.

Twist Stance: Bend the leading leg slightly and place 99 percent of your weight on that leg. The rear leg crosses behind this leg with the foot resting on the ball such that the toes point toward the outside edge of the supporting foot. Like the tiger stance, this is not a particularly mobile stance. Its primary use is as an intermediate posture that the student uses in preparation for changing direction of motion or for launching a kick.

Walking Stance: Step forward a distance of one shoulder width with the lead foot while shifting the hips forward so that weight is distributed with 70 percent supported by the front leg and 30 percent supported by the rear leg. The toes of the leading foot should point directly to the front while the toes of the rear leg point outward 45 degrees. When properly set, you should appear to have frozen in mid-stride. This is a fairly mobile stance that can be useful in all combat situations. The major benefit of this stance is that while it allows mobility, the placement of more than half of the body's weight on the lead leg allows you to execute quick and powerful rear-foot kicks.

Tiger Stance: Bend the rear leg (without lifting the heel from the floor) and put 99 percent of your weight on that leg. Raise the front foot up on the ball and slide it close in front of the rear leg. Knees are pulled together to protect lower body areas, specifically the groin. Although not as mobile a stance, this stance is stable for defensive maneuvers and allows quick kicks with leading foot. This is a defensive stance only. It's not useful for offensive tactics.

Kicking Stance: Stand with feet approximately shoulder width apart (A). From here, turn both feet approximately 45 degrees to the side (B), and slide the rear foot back slightly more than one shoulder width distance (C). The rear foot should be raised slightly on the ball, and both knees should be bent comfortably. As in the back stance, the chest is turned 45 degrees from the forward direction, thereby offering a narrower target to the opponent. This is Tae Kwon Do's most versatile stance and is generally used in combat/sparring situations.

The most important thing to remember about stances is that while each has specific uses, to remain rigidly posed in any stance is to make your movements stiff and mechanical. The kicking stance is the stance you would begin with in virtually every combat or sparring situation. Keep your weight on the balls of your feet at all times and keep moving by bouncing lightly with a steady rhythm. From here, you will be able to flow into the various stances as needed in a given situation. Remember, *never* stand still.

BLOCKS

A   B

Rising Block: Cross both arms in front of the body (A), then thrust the blocking arm upward in front of the face until it stops approximately one fist's distance above the top of the head with the forearm angling upward at about 45 degrees (B). At the same time, the nonblocking arm is retracted into position at your belt.* Note that the forearm, which is the blocking surface, covers the entire head area. This is a defense against a downward attack to the head and shoulders or a direct attack to the face.

A   B

Down Block: The blocking arm is first raised to the opposite side of the head with the palm turned toward the ear (A), then swept down and across the front of the body to stop with the fist before the center of your belt and the forearm angling downward at approximately 45 degrees (B). The blocking surface is the outer forearm. The technique is a defense against attacks to the middle and lower sections of the body.

---

* You will notice throughout this chapter that in many cases the nonblocking or striking hand is drawn back into position at the belt at the same time that the technique is executed. Whenever the rear hand is not directly useful in delivering a technique, the counteraction of retracting that hand toward the belt helps to drive power into the block/ strike. This is one of the central features of Tae Kwon Do and an important means of generating maximum power in a technique.

X Block: Draw both hands back into position at the side of the body, then shoot arms forward at the same time to cross at the wrists. The blocking surface is the area between the wrists where the forearms cross. Illustrations (A,B) show a high X block, and illustrations (C,D) show a low X block. The low X block is a defense against attacks to the lower body, in particular the groin, while the high X block is a defense against downward attacks to the head and shoulders and attacks to the face.

Inner Arm Block: Raise your bent arm to the side of the head (A), then swing it forward and to the inside (B) until the forearm crosses before your face to stop in line with the opposite shoulder (C). The blocking surface is the outer forearm bone. This is a defense against direct oncoming attacks to the head and upper body.

Outer Arm Block: Extend the blocking arm straight across the front of your body (A), then swing it upward and in front of your face (B) until the arm stops with forearm in line with the shoulder of that arm (C). The blocking surface is the inner forearm bone. This is a defense against direct oncoming attacks to the face and upper body.

Reverse Outer Arm Block: Bring blocking arm to opposite side of head (A), then swing forearm across face B) until arm stops in line with the same shoulder (C). Note that the palm is returned away from the face. Blocking surface is the outer forearm bone. This is a defense against direct oncoming attacks to the face.

A   B   C   D

Knife-Hand Block: Blocking hand forms a knife-hand position[*] and is brought to the opposite side of the head (A), then snapped out to cross in front of the face and stop palm out with the hand in line with that shoulder (B). Blocking surface is the edge of the hand. This is a defense against direct oncoming attacks to the face and upper body. This technique may also be performed to protect the lower body areas, as in illustrations (C,D).

A   B   C   D

Double Knife-Hand Block: Both hands form knife-hands as blocking hand is brought up beside the head while the rear hand is extended to the back (A), then both hands are swung forward so that the lead hand stops palm out in line with the shoulder as the rear hand stops palm up before the solar plexus (B). Blocking surface is the edge of the lead hand. This technique is a defense against direct oncoming attacks to the head and upper body with additional covering protection for the solar plexus provided by the rear hand. This technique may also be performed to protect the lower areas, as in illustrations (C,D).

[*] See the following section on strikes for instructions to make a proper knife hand.

A B

Palm Block: Blocking hand is held open in knife-hand position and brought to shoulder level (A), then thrust inward to stop before the center line of the body (B). Blocking surface is the palm. This technique is a defense against direct oncoming attacks to the center of the body.

STRIKES

It's absolutely essential that every student of Tae Kwon Do master proper hand positioning. This will prevent injury to the hands, and aid in the effective delivery of power. The five basic hand positions we will cover here are the fist, knife-hand, ridge hand, spear fingers and knuckle-fist.

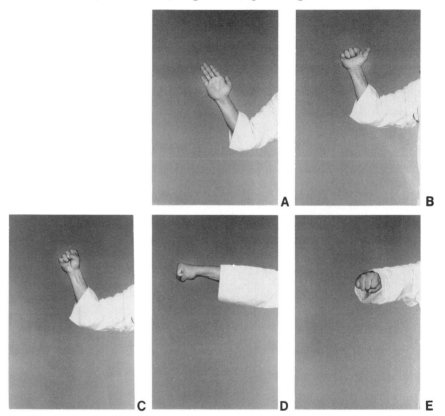

The Tae Kwon Do Fist: The important points to remember in making a proper fist are, first, that the fingers must be closed tightly so that there is no opening inside and, second, that the thumb is strongly clenched against the underside of the first two fingers. The reason for preventing open space within the fist is to insure that the fingers do not give at the moment of impact, which will lead to injury. Similarly, the thumb must be tightly tucked in to prevent its being caught on something during a strike and pulled back and broken. Further, with the thumb tucked tightly against the first two fingers, those fingers are made especially immobile and strong. This is important because the power of a punch is focused on the first two knuckles of the fist (see illustration (E)). Following the illustrations, we begin to make a proper fist by beginning with an open hand (A), which is then closed by curling the fingers into the palm (B), and finally clasping the thumb tightly against the first two fingers (C). From the side, the fist makes a straight extension of the forearm, with the wrist bent neither up nor down (D). This is critical! If the wrist is even slightly bent either up or down when a punch is thrown, a broken wrist will almost surely be the result. As viewed from straight on (E), it can be seen that the first two knuckles of the fist are naturally larger and therefore stronger than those of the other fingers, which are unsupported, forming a powerful striking surface.

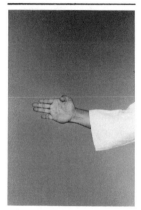

The Knife-Hand: The knife-hand is formed quite easily by pressing the fingers of the open hand together, with the tips of the fingers curled inward (without cupping the hands), while the thumb is bent and held tightly against the side of the hand. The ends of the fingers are curled inward as described here to prevent the fingers from being broken in the event that the fingertips are hit directly. In this way the fingers will curl in to the palm and not backward. The same is true of the thumb being flexed and held tightly against the hand. This prevents the finger from being caught and broken. The striking surface of the knife-hand is the "blade" edge of the hand.

The Ridge-Hand: The ridge-hand is formed similar to the knife-hand except that the striking surface is the edge of the hand where the thumb is. To prevent damage to the thumb, it is tucked into the palm to form a flat striking surface.

The Spear Fingers: The spear fingers position is also similar to the knife-hand, however, the striking surface of this technique is the tips of the fingers themselves. As with the knife-hand, the tips of the fingers are flexed slightly to prevent injury.

The Knuckle-Fist: The knuckle-fist is formed by closing the hand into a proper fist and then extending the middle finger forward so that the second knuckle projects in front of the others. This extended knuckle then becomes the striking surface. Note that the tip of the thumb supports the second finger.

A   B   C   D

Straight Punching: The power delivered by a Tae Kwon Do punch depends greatly on the correctness of form when that punch is delivered. To practice this type of punching, we strongly advise punching from a horseback riding stance as illustrated. This type of punching is only for drilling purposes to perfect your punching technique—it's not a sparring technique. The openness of the horseback riding stance from the front will place the student at a great disadvantage if the stance is used in a combat situation.

To practice straight punching, assume a horseback riding stance as illustrated in (A) and extend one fist in front of your body. Note that the fist is placed at a point in the center of the body and not simply extended straight out from the shoulder. This is to develop an instinct for centering a punch on target. Notice also that the arm which is not extended is drawn back to the belt. This position is known as chamber. Next, the rear hand is driven forward as the lead arm is retracted (B), and this motion continues as the hands pass each other (C), until the hands have changed position (D). Note that the hands twist as they move so that once fully extended, the punching hand is palm down while the rear hand is palm up. This twisting motion of the hands aids in the delivery of power by allowing the arm to move naturally. If the hands were maintained in a palm down position throughout the entire motion of the strike, the arm would be twisted in an unnatural position when the hand is retracted to the belt.

Side Punch: From an upright standing position the striking arm is pulled tightly into chamber as your body twists in the direction the strike is to be delivered while the leading foot is lifted from the floor (A). Next the lead leg steps out (B) and the arm is fully extended into position straight from the shoulder and parallel to the floor (C). Note that for the purposes of depicting the technique we have broken the technique into distinct segments. However, when actually performing this technique, there should be no pause between (B) and (C).

Jab Punch: This technique is used to strike an opponent quickly as a distraction, or as a set up for a finishing technique. Quite simply, a jab punch is a straight punch delivered with the leading hand. From guard position (A) the lead hand is snapped out quickly to strike the target (B)(C). Note that the weight is not shifted forward significantly during the strike.

A   **B**   **C**   **D**

Reverse Punch: The reverse punch is the single most powerful hand-striking technique in Tae Kwon Do. Essentially, a reverse punch is a straight punch delivered with the rear hand. The power of this technique, however, comes from the way the hips are shifted into the blow, combined with the torquing of the upper body and the momentary snapping of the shoulders into position at the moment of impact. From the normal guard position in (A), the hips are twisted forward so that the knot of the belt points at the target (B). The striking hand is then snapped out and extended into the target (C) (D). Note how the weight is shifted forward here, with the shoulders turned at the moment of the strike, and how the rear foot is raised high on the ball to drive power into the strike.

A   **B**   **C**   **D**

Double Punch: The double punch is a combination punch merging both the jab and reverse punches. From the normal guard position the lead hand is first snapped out in a jab (A,B), followed immediately by a reverse punch with the rear hand (C,D). Since speed is the primary concern here, it is important to note that the nonstriking hand is not retracted to the belt but remains in position to protect the body. This is a very useful technique in sparring situations where the initial jab punch opens up the opponent for the finishing blow of the reverse punch.

Knife-Hand Strike: The knife-hand strike uses the edge of the hand to deliver the force of the blow. (Although here we have shown only the basic attack to the neck, the knife-hand strike can be delivered in many directions). With the striking hand held in the proper knife-hand position, the hand is brought close to the side of the head (A), then swung outward as the arm straightens (B), until the blow is landed (C). Note that at the moment of the strike, the striking arm is not completely straight but remains slightly bent. A perfectly straight arm will not be able to deliver the same force and the shock of the blow may injure the elbow.

Spear Fingers Strike: With the striking hand held in the proper spear fingers position, the arm is retracted to *chamber* position (A) and then the striking hand is thrust forward (B), until the arm straightens to thrust the fingertips into the target (C). Caution must be exercised before attempting this technique. Years of practice and conditioning must be undertaken before using this technique or serious injury to the fingers can result.

KICKS

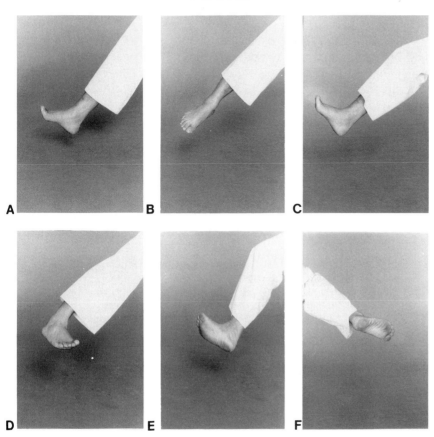

The striking surfaces: Before actually touching on the kicking techniques themselves, however, it is important that we first show the proper ways in which the foot can be held as well as the various striking surfaces of the foot. There are six basic areas used in delivering strikes: the ball of the foot (A); the instep (B); the heel (C), both the back and bottom; the blade edge of the foot (D); the arch (E); and the sole of the foot (F). Look carefully at how the foot is positioned when striking with each of the various surfaces. For more detailed explanations of when particular surfaces of the foot are used, you will need to study the following illustrations, which depict the different types of kicks. (Note: although we will show all of the kicks in this section from a kicking stance alone, it is important to remember that any kick can be performed from virtually any other stance as well, in particular the front and back stances, depending on the actual situation.)

The kicking techniques of Tae Kwon Do are the most powerful means of delivering blows in this, and indeed any martial art system. Kicks are more powerful than arm strikes because the leg has almost four times the mass of muscle as the arm. For the average person, however, the muscles of the legs are far too tight to be used effectively to strike with. They find it all but impossible to reach out with their feet in the same, easy, controlled manner that a practiced student of Tae Kwon Do is able to display. Only by working many years to stretch the muscles of the legs, and by learning the proper ways in which to use their hips and body mass, can students of the art learn to make use of the power in their legs and feet. Once the kicks have been mastered, they can be delivered with devastating results. It is this emphasis on kicking techniques that makes Tae Kwon Do so unique and so effective. The kicks that we have illustrated here represent all the basic types of kicks to be found in Tae Kwon Do. As you study the pictures, pay careful attention to the way in which the hips are used to drive power into each kick. Power can be developed only by learning how to shift your weight and align your pelvis properly.

A   B   C   D

Side Kick: The side kick is the single most powerful kicking technique in Tae Kwon Do. The drive provided by the supporting leg, combined with the proper aligning of the hips, generates tremendous power in this kick. The knee of the kicking leg is first raised with the heel tucked into the buttocks (A). Next, the hips shift slightly as the foot is raised (B) with the bottom of the heel aimed at the target. Finally, the leg is straightened toward the target, driving the heel into it (C,D). Note the position of the supporting foot, with the toes pointing 180 degrees away from the target. Turning the foot in this way aligns the hips properly to drive added power into this technique.

A   B   C

Roundhouse Kick: The objective of the roundhouse kick is to deliver a blow from a 90 degree angle to the target. Study the illustrations here carefully to see how this is accomplished. First, the kicking foot is raised to the side with the knee bent (A). Then the leg is straightened to swing the foot around at the target (B), until the leg has been fully extended and the blow landed (C). The striking surface used for this kick is the instep. Note how the hips are shifted forward during the kick. This shifting of weight is very important in the generation of power in the technique. If the hips remain back, the range and power of the kick will be severely limited.

A   B

Rising Kick: Although we have included this technique under the section on kicks, this is not a combat technique. Rather, this kick serves the purpose of an exercise, assisting in the development of stretch and leg strength. The kicking leg is raised quickly to the front as high as possible, with the foot flexed and the toes pulled back (A,B). It is important to note that the knee remains straight throughout the entire motion of the kick.

A   B   C   D

Front Kick: The knee of the kicking leg is first raised and pointed at the intended target (A), then the leg is snapped out and quickly straightened into the target (B). The usual striking surfaces for this kick are either the instep or the ball of the foot (C, D).

A   B   C

D   E   F

Crossing Kick: The crossing kick is another technique for delivering a blow at a right angle to the target. With the kicking leg extended, the foot is raised and swung in an arc across the front of the body to strike the target with the blade edge of the foot for an inside to outside crossing kick, as illustrated in (A, B, C), or with the arch of the foot for an outside to inside crossing kick, as illustrated in (D, E, F).

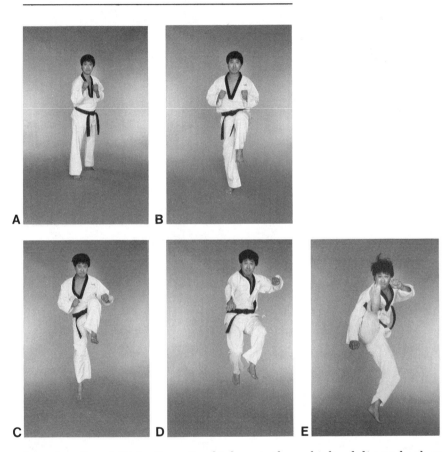

Jumping Front Kick: Jumping kicks are those kicks delivered when neither foot is in contact with the floor. In Tae Kwon Do there are also kicks known collectively as flying kicks. Like jumping kicks, these are done with both feet off the floor, but during a flying kick the objective is to cover distance horizontally and not simply to jump straight up and down. Flying kicks will not be shown here, but the form is identical to that of jumping kicks after taking a few running steps.

For the jumping front kick, bring the rear leg forward and up (A,B), raising the knee powerfully to help give lift. Once the supporting foot leaves the ground, that foot is brought up quickly to deliver the kick in the same manner as a standing front snap kick (C, D, E).

A   B   C   D

Hook Kick: The hook kick may be considered a reverse application of the roundhouse kick. The kicking foot is raised with the knee bent and drawn across the front of the body (A). Then the foot is swung upward in an arc (B) to bring the heel across and into the target (C,D). The foot should not arc across the target at the moment of impact, but travel in a straight line parallel to the floor for maximum effectiveness. This is accomplished by turning the hips fully into the kick as the leg extends.

A   B   C   D

Spinning Back Kick: Unlike the preceding kicks that delivered blows to the front of the body, the spinning back kick is unique in that with it you strike to the rear. First, step forward with the back leg and spin quickly to look over your shoulder as pictured here (A,B). The kicking leg is then raised (C), and the foot is thrust out to the rear to drive the heel into the target (D).

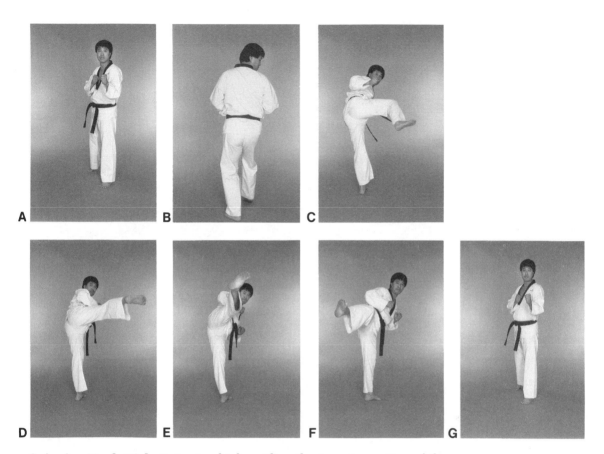

Spinning Hook Kick: Spinning kicks utilize the torquing action of the body to assist in developing power in a kick. The first of the two kicks we have included here is the spinning hook kick. This is identical to the normal hook kick, with the exception that the user first spins quickly on one foot before the kicking leg is extended. From a kicking stance (A), begin by shifting your weight to the front leg and spinning quickly in the direction of your rear side (B). As you spin, raise the kicking leg and look over your shoulder at the target (C). This is particularly important—you must first see the target before you can land the kick. Note that the supporting foot settles firmly into position (with toes pointing 180 degrees away from the target) as the kicking leg lashes out. This helps to provide stability. From here, the motion of the kick is identical to that of the normal hook kick (D,E,F). Following the delivery of the kick, however, the spin is completed, so that you return to the starting position (G).

Axe Kick: The axe kick uses the rear of the heel to deliver a blow straight downward. The kicking foot is swung up across the body (A), until it is high in the air (B), when it is brought straight down onto the target (C).

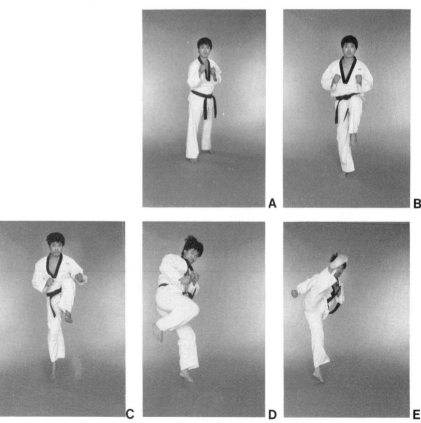

Jumping Round Kick: The jumping round kick is performed in much the same manner as the jumping front snap kick. The rear leg is brought forward and up (A,B) to help provide lift, then the rear leg cocks and swings around to deliver the kick once you are in the air (C, D, E).

Jumping Side Kick: as with the preceding kicks, the rear leg helps to thrust the body into the air (A,B) where you bring up the kicking foot and execute the kick (C,D,E). Note that to perform a jumping side kick properly, the body must twist to the side in midair so that the hips can be brought into proper alignment.

While the preceding illustrations represent all of the basic techniques of Tae Kwon Do, there are many ways in which they are used. Strikes and kicks are delivered from various combinations of quick spins and jumps, as well as from a far wider variety of stances than only the basic positions we have shown here. We will touch upon these further methods of delivering kicks in Chapter 4, where we discuss sparring techniques in greater depth. Our intention here, however, is merely to show in detail the proper ways in which kicks, strikes, blocks and stances are executed.

These are the building blocks of the art and must become instinctive if a student hopes to gain proficiency. Just as the foundation of a house must be properly set for the structure to be strong, so too is it necessary for students to have a firm grasp of the basic techniques if their sparring skills are to be strong and effective.

3
FORMS

Putting It All Together

More than any other exercise or drill, the practice of forms is the most important element in the development of proper Tae Kwon Do technique. Required for advancement at every level from beginner through master, forms serve a multidimensional role, aiding in the development and refinement of coordination, balance, timing, breath control and rhythm, all of which are essential skills to the Tae Kwon Do student. Students are taught one form at each successive belt level, beginning with the white belt level (which indicates a novice student). When a student has mastered the specific form for his belt level and has demonstrated an increased proficiency with the basic techniques, he is ready to advance to the next level.

Through the practice of forms, which require students to strike and kick in different directions, block and attack in a coordinated manner, and change directions suddenly, students quickly develop the skilled instincts necessary in Tae Kwon Do. Although students of the art must master far more than the specific form required at their current belt level to advance to higher rank, the repeated practice of forms will enable even the novice to develop a fairly sophisticated combat technique. This is by no means surprising because it was for this very reason that masters developed forms over the years.

Forms, or *poomse* in Korean, are a series of defending and attacking movements performed against imaginary opponents in a set pattern. Through the practice of forms, students come to learn the applications of the various techniques of Tae Kwon Do. The movements of each form have been carefully arranged by the masters to teach students effective methods for dealing with a wide array of attacks from all possible directions, with particular emphasis placed on the equal development of both sides of the body. It is essential in Tae Kwon Do for students to become equally proficient in defending or attacking from both the left and right side of the body as the situation demands. Often, an entire series of techniques will be mirrored within a form to emphasize the importance of proficiency with both sides of the body. Although every student ultimately develops his own "favorite side," the ability to react effectively to either side becomes deeply ingrained through the practice of forms until it is instinctive.

In addition, forms teach Tae Kwon Do students the proper way in which each technique (i.e., punches, kicks, blocks, etc.) is executed. Under the supervision of a qualified instructor, students learn how to use their entire bodies to deliver the power of a technique to a specific point in space. The ability to do this is called focus. We will discuss it in detail in Chapter 6. It is focus that gives masters of Tae Kwon Do their tremendous power. Blocks, strikes, kicks, balance and tension movements are all strung together into a pattern that, when performed properly, flows in a graceful and powerful choreography.

The primary forms of Tae Kwon Do are known as the *Tae Geuk* series and are studied by all students below the level of black belt. These eight forms are now the only forms sanctioned by the Korean Tae Kwon Do Association for rank advancement in the art. Over the years, other groups of forms have been used in the teaching of Tae Kwon Do, the most widespread being the Pyung-Ahn series and the Pal Gwe series. Although some of these systems can trace their roots back to early Korean masters, virtually all of them showed evidence of Chinese and/or Japanese influence. In a move to standardize the forms of Tae Kwon Do, the Korean Tae Kwon Do Association authorized the formulation of the new Tae Geuk system, making all other forms obsolete.

On the following pages, each of these forms has been broken down into individual movements to illustrate clearly the overall pattern. The direction of movement is indicated by the line and arrow diagram beside each picture. As a point of reference, the camera angle will always be from the same direction (with the exception of certain illustrations taken from an angle of 180 degrees opposite from the normal camera angle to show the details of certain movements that would otherwise be done facing away from the camera). Along with a description of each movement we have included a brief explanation of the meaning of each technique. Collectively, the pictures, diagrams and explanations divide each of the forms into distinct parts that can be studied in detail. It is important to remember, however, that although we have broken the forms down into distinct parts, there are many subtleties to each form (such as timing and rhythm) which cannot be learned from a book. These important features can only be learned under the guidance of a qualified instructor.

The Tae Geuk forms were devised based on the ideals of the *Jooyeok (Book of Changes),* a highly revered philosophical work that puts forward profound perspectives on life, the world and the universe. The Tae Geuk system was carefully crafted to serve as a physical expression of the essence of the *Jooyeok.* Translated literally, *Tae* means "bigness" and *Geuk* means "eternity"—in other words, that which has no form, no beginning or ending. Yet the concept of Tae Geuk includes the understanding that it is also the source of everything. From this central concept, eight major branches of philosophical thought have been devised. Thus each of the eight Tae Geuk Poomse (formal exercises or forms) is based on one of these aspects. Through physical action, a student's balance, coordination, breath control and direction of energy are harmoniously blended in a choreography that reflects the eight aspects of the universe.

TAE GEUK FORM ONE

Tae Geuk El-Jong

Movement 1: turn 90° left, moving left foot out into a left walking stance facing toward D and execute a left arm low block.

Meaning: defense against an attack to the middle section of the body.

Movement 2: step forward with right foot into a right walking stance and punch with right fist to middle section.

Meaning: counterattack by defender.

Movement 3: turn 180° right, step with right foot into a right walking stance facing C and execute a right arm low block.

Meaning: defense against an attack to the middle section of the body.

Movement 4: step forward with left foot into a left walking stance and punch with left fist to middle section.

Meaning: counterattack by defender.

Movement 5a: step 90° left with left foot into a left forward stance facing B and execute a left arm low block.

Meaning: defense against an attack to the low section of the body.

Movement 5b: remain in same stance and execute a punch to the middle section with the right fist.

Meaning: immediate counterattack by defender.

Movement 6: step 90° right with right foot into a right walking stance facing E and execute a middle block to the inside using the left arm.

Meaning: defense against an attack to the middle section.

Movement 7: step forward with left foot into a left walking stance and punch to middle section with right fist.

Meaning: counterattack by defender.

Movement 8: step 180° left with left foot into a left walking stance facing F and execute a middle block to the inside using the right arm.

Meaning: defense against an attack to the middle section.

Movement 9: step forward with right foot into a right walking stance and execute a middle section punch with left fist.

Meaning: counterattack by defender.

Movement 10a: step 90° right with right foot into a right forward stance facing B and execute a low block with right arm.

Meaning: defense against an attack to the lower section of the body.

Movement 10b: remain in same stance and execute a middle section punch with left fist.

Meaning: immediate counterattack by defender.

Movement 11: step 90° left into a left walking stance facing H and execute a rising block with left arm.

Meaning: defense against a downward attack to the head.

Movement 12a: keeping left foot in place, execute a middle section front kick with right foot.

Meaning: initial counterattack by defender.

Movement 12b: step down with right foot into a right walking stance and execute a middle section punch with right fist.

Meaning: finishing counterattack by defender.

Movement 13: step 180° right into a right walking stance facing G and execute a rising block with right arm.

Meaning: defense against a downward attack to the head.

Movement 14a: keeping right foot in place, execute a middle section front kick with left foot.

Meaning: initial counterattack by defender.

Movement 14b: step down with left foot into a left walking stance and execute a middle section punch with left fist.

Meaning: finishing counterattack by defender.

Movement 15: step 90° right with left foot into a left forward stance facing A and execute a low block with left arm.

Meaning: defense against low section attack.

Front view.

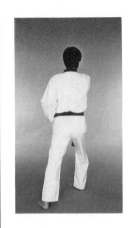

Movement 16: step forward with right foot into a right forward stance and execute a middle section punch with right fist. Yell, "Ki hop!"

Meaning: strong counterattack by defender.

Front view.

Finish form by turning 180° left, pivoting on right foot to end by facing B in a ready stance.

TAE GEUK FORM TWO

Tae Geuk E-Jong

Movement 1: step 90° left into a left walking stance facing D and execute a down block with left arm.

Meaning: defense against an attack to the middle section.

Movement 2: step forward with right foot into a right forward stance while executing a middle section punch with the right fist.

Meaning: counterattack by defender.

Movement 3: turn 180° right into a right walking stance facing C and execute a low block with right arm.

Meaning: defense against an attack to the middle section.

Movement 4: step forward with left foot into a left forward stance and execute a middle section punch with the left fist.

Meaning: counterattack by defender.

Movement 5: turn 90° left into a left walking stance facing B and execute an inside forearm block with right arm.

Meaning: defense against an attack to the upper section.

Movement 6: step forward with right foot into a right walking stance and execute an inside forearm block with left arm.

Meaning: defense against an attack to the upper section.

Movement 7: turn 90° left into a left walking stance facing F and execute a down block with left arm.

Meaning: defense against an attack to the lower section.

Movement 8a: execute a front kick to the middle section with right foot.

Movement 8b: step down with right foot into a right forward stance and execute a high section punch with right fist.

Meaning: double counterattack by defender.

Movement 9: turn 180° right into a right walking stance facing E and execute a down block with right arm.

Meaning: defense against an attack to the middle section.

Movement 10a: execute a front kick to the middle section with left foot.

Movement 10b: step down with left foot into a left forward stance and execute a high section punch with left fist.

Meaning: double counterattack by defender.

Movement 11: turn 90° left into a left walking stance facing B and execute a rising block with the left arm.

Meaning: defense against a downward attack to the head.

Movement 12: step forward with right foot into a right walking stance and execute a rising block with the right arm.

Meaning: defense against a downward attack to the head.

Movement 13: turn 270° left into a left walking stance facing G and execute an inside forearm block with right arm.

Meaning: defense against an attack to the middle section.

Movement 14: turn 180° right into a right walking stance facing H and execute an inside forearm block with right arm.

Meaning: defense against an attack to the middle section.

Movement 15: turn 90° left into a left walking stance facing A and execute a down block with left arm.

Meaning: defense against an attack to the middle section.

Front view.

Movement 16a: execute a middle section front kick with right foot.

Front view.

Movement 16b: step down with right foot into a right walking stance and execute a middle section punch with right fist.

Meaning: double counterattack by defender.

Front view.

Movement 17a: execute a middle section front kick with left foot.

Front view.

Movement 17b: step down with left foot into a left walking stance and execute a middle section punch with left hand.

Meaning: double counterattack by defender.

Front view.

Movement 18a: execute a middle section front kick with right foot.

Front view.

Movement 18b: step down with right foot into a right walking stance and execute a middle section punch with right hand. Yell, "Ki hop!"

Meaning: double counterattack by defender.

Front view.

TAE GEUK FORM THREE

Tae Geuk Sam-Jong

Movement 1: turn 90° left into a left walking stance facing D and execute a down block with left arm.

Meaning: defense against an attack to middle section.

Movement 2a: execute a middle section front kick with right foot.

Movement 2b: step down with right foot into a right forward stance and execute two middle section punches in rapid succession, right hand first.

Movement 2c: . . . followed by left hand.

Meaning: multiple counterattack by defender.

Movement 3: Turn 180° right into a right walking stance facing C and execute a down block with right arm.

Meaning: defense against an attack to the middle section.

Movement 4a: execute a middle section front kick with left foot.

Movement 4b: step down with left foot into a left forward stance and execute two middle section punches in rapid succession, left hand first.

Movement 4c: . . . followed by right hand.

Meaning: multiple counterattack by defender.

Movement 5: turn 90° left into a left walking stance facing B and execute an inward knife-hand strike to high section (side of neck) with right hand.

Meaning: defender takes offensive against attacker.

Movement 6: step forward into right walking stance and execute an inward knife-hand strike to high section with left hand.

Meaning: defender continues with offensive against attacker.

Movement 7: turn 90° left into back stance facing F and execute a knife-hand block with left hand.

Meaning: defense against an attack to the middle section.

Movement 8: step forward with left foot into a left forward stance and execute a middle section punch with right hand.

Meaning: counterattack by defender.

Movement 9: turn 180° right into a right back stance facing E and execute a knife-hand block with right hand.

Meaning: defense against an attack to the middle section.

Movement 10: step forward with right foot into a right forward stance and execute a middle section punch with left hand.

Meaning: counterattack by defender.

Movement 11: turn 90° left into a left walking stance facing B and execute an inward forearm block with right arm.

Meaning: defense against an attack to the middle section.

Movement 12: step forward with right foot into a right walking stance and execute an inner forearm block using left arm.

Meaning: defense against an attack to the middle section.

Movement 13: turn 270° left into a left walking stance facing G and execute an inside forearm block with right arm.

Meaning: defense against an attack to the middle section.

Movement 14a: execute a middle section front kick with right foot.

Movement 14b: step down with right foot into a right forward stance and execute two middle section punches in rapid succession, right hand first.

Movement 14c: . . . followed by left.

Meaning: multiple counterattack by defender.

Movement 15: turn 180° right into a right walking stance facing H and execute a down block with right arm.

Meaning: defense against an attack to the middle section.

Movement 16a: execute a middle section front kick with left foot.

Movement 16b: step down with left foot into a left forward stance and execute two middle section punches in rapid succession, left hand first.

Movement 16c: . . . then right hand.

Meaning: multiple counterattack by defender.

Movement 17a: turn 90° left into a left walking stance facing A and execute a down block with left arm.

Front view.

Movement 17b: follow down block immediately with middle section punch with right hand.

Meaning: simultaneous middle section block and counterattack by defender.

Front view.

Movement 18a: step forward with right foot into a right walking stance and execute a down block with right arm (front view).

Movement 18b: follow down block immediately with middle section punch with left hand (front view).

Meaning: simultaneous middle section block and counterattack by defender.

Movement 19a: execute a middle section front kick with left foot (front view).

Movement 19b: step down with left foot into a left walking stance and execute a down block with left arm (front view).

Movement 19c: follow down block immediately with middle section punch with right hand (front view).

Meaning: defender takes offensive against attacker.

Movement 20a: execute a middle section front kick with right foot (front view).

Movement 20b: step down with right foot into a right walking stance and execute a down block with right arm (front view).

Movement 20c: follow down block immediately with middle section punch with left hand (front view). Yell, "Ki hop!"

TAE GEUK FORM FOUR

Tae Geuk Sa-Jong

Movement 1: turn 90° left into a left back stance facing D and execute a double knife-hand block.

Meaning: defense against an attack to the middle section.

Movement 2: step forward with right foot into a forward stance and execute a palm block with the left hand followed immediately with a middle target spear-hand strike.

Meaning: simultaneous block and counterattack by defender.

Movement 3: turn 180° right into a back stance facing C and execute a double knife-hand block.

Meaning: defense against an attack to the middle section.

Movement 4: step forward with left foot into a front stance and execute a palm block with the right hand followed immediately with a middle target spear-hand strike.

Meaning: simultaneous block and counterattack by defender.

Movement 5: turn 90° left into a left forward stance facing B and execute a knife-hand rising block with left hand and simultaneous high section strike with right knife-hand.

Meaning: simultaneous block and counterattack by defender.

Movement 6a: execute a middle section front snap kick with right foot.

Meaning: defender takes offensive.

Movement 6b: step down with right foot into a right forward stance and execute a middle section punch with left fist.

Meaning: defender continues to take the offensive.

Movement 7: execute a middle section side kick with left foot.

Meaning: defender presses offensive and forces opponent back.

Movement 8a: step down with left foot and turn quickly to execute a middle section side kick with right foot.

Meaning: defender continues to press opponent back.

Movement 8b: step down with right foot into a right back stance and execute a double knife-hand block.

Meaning: defense against an attack to the middle section.

Movement 9: turn 270° left into a left back stance facing G and execute an outer arm block with left arm.

Meaning: defense against an attack to the middle section.

Movement 10a: execute a middle section front kick with right foot.

Meaning: counterattack by defender.

Movement 10b: step back with right foot into a left back stance and execute an inner arm block with right arm.

Meaning: defense against an attack to the middle section.

Movement 11: turn 180° right into a right back stance facing H and execute an outer arm block with right arm.

Meaning: defense against an attack to the middle section.

Movement 12a: execute a middle section front kick with the left foot.

Meaning: counterattack by defender.

Movement 12b: step back with left foot into a right back stance and execute an inner arm block with the left arm.

Meaning: defense against an attack to the middle section.

Movement 13: turn 90° left into a left front stance facing A and execute a knife-hand rising block with the left hand and a simultaneous high section strike with the right knife-hand (front view).

Meaning: simultaneous block and attack by defender.

Movement 14a: execute a middle section front kick with right foot (front view).

Meaning: defender takes the offensive.

Movement 14b: step down with right foot into right front stance facing A and execute a high section strike with right back fist (front view).

Meaning: defender lands finishing blow.

Movement 15: turn 90° left into a left walking stance facing E and execute an inner arm block using left arm.

Meaning: defense against an attack to the middle section.

Movement 16: execute a middle section punch with right fist.

Meaning: counterattack by defender.

Movement 17: turn 180° right into a right walking stance facing F and execute an inner arm block using the right arm.

Meaning: defense against an attack to the middle section.

Movement 18: execute a middle section punch with left arm.

Meaning: counterattack by defender.

Movement 19a: turn 90° left into a left front stance facing A and execute an inner arm block using the left arm (front view).

Meaning: defense against an attack to the middle section.

Movement 19b: remain in same stance and execute two middle section punches, right fist first (front view).

Movement 19c: followed by left fist (front view).

Meaning: double counterattack by defender.

Movement 20a: step forward with right foot into a right forward stance and execute an inner arm block using the right arm (front view).

Meaning: defense against an attack to the middle section.

Movement 20b: remain in same stance and execute two middle target punches, left fist first (front view).

Movement 20c: . . . followed by right fist (front view). Yell, "Ki hop!"

Meaning: double counterattack by defender.

TAE GEUK FORM FIVE

Tae Geuk O-Jong

Movement 1: turn 90° left into a left forward stance facing D and execute a down block with left arm.

Meaning: defense against an attack to the lower section.

Movement 2: slide left foot back into an open stance and execute a downward hammer-fist strike with left hand.

Meaning: counterattack by defender.

Movement 3: turn body 180° right into a forward stance facing C and execute a down block with right arm.

Meaning: defense against an attack to the lower section.

Movement 4: slide right foot back into an open stance and execute a downward hammer-fist strike with right hand.

Meaning: counterattack by defender.

Movement 5a: step forward with left foot forming a front stance facing B and execute an inner arm block with left arm.

Movement 5b: remain in same stance and immediately execute a second inner arm block with right arm.

Meaning: defense against a double attack to the middle section.

Movement 6a: execute a middle section front kick with right foot.

Movement 6b: step down with right foot into a right forward stance and execute a high section back-fist strike with right hand.

Movement 6c: remain in same stance and execute an inner arm block with left arm.

Meaning: defender takes offensive.

Movement 7a: execute a middle section front kick with left foot.

Movement 7b: step down with left foot into a left forward stance and execute a high section back-fist strike with left hand.

Movement 7c: remain in same stance and execute an inner arm block with right arm.

Meaning: defender continues to take offensive.

Movement 8: step forward with right foot (stamping on floor) forming a right forward stance and execute a high section back-fist strike with right hand.

Meaning: finishing attack by defender.

Movement 9: turn 270° left into a left back stance facing G and execute a knife-hand block with left hand.

Meaning: defense against an attack to the middle section.

Movement 10: cover knuckles of right fist with left knife-hand, step forward with right foot into a right forward stance and execute a middle section elbow strike with right elbow.

Meaning: counterattack by defender.

Movement 11: turn 180° right into a right back stance facing H and execute a knife-hand block with right hand.

Meaning: defense against an attack to the middle section.

Movement 12: cover knuckles of left fist with right knife-hand, step forward with left foot into a left forward stance and execute a middle section elbow strike with left elbow.

Meaning: counterattack by defender.

Movement 13a: turn 90° left into a left forward stance facing A and execute a down block with left arm (front view).

Movement 13b: remain in same stance and execute an inner block with right arm (front view).

Meaning: double defense: first, against an attack to the lower section, and second, to the middle section.

Movement 14a: execute a middle section front kick with right foot (front view).

Movement 14b: step down with right foot into a right forward stance and execute a down block with right arm (front view).

Movement 14c: remain in same stance and execute an inner arm block with left arm (front view).

Meaning: defender takes offensive with kick and defends against two attacks by opponent: first, to the lower section, and second, to the middle section.

Movement 15: turn 90° left into a left forward stance facing E and execute a rising block with left arm.

Meaning: defense against a downward strike to the head.

Movement 16a: execute a middle section side kick with right foot.

C ———— A ———— D

E ←———— F

G ———— H
          B

Movement 16b: step down with right foot into a right forward stance and execute a left elbow strike to palm of right hand.

Meaning: double counterattack by defender.

C ———— A ———— D

E ←———— F

G ———— H
          B

Movement 17: turn 180° right into a right forward stance facing F and execute a rising block with right arm.

Meaning: defense against a downward attack to the head.

C ———— A ———— D

E ————→ F

G ———— H
          B

Movement 18a: execute a middle section side kick with left foot.

Movement 18b: step down with left foot into a left forward stance and execute a right elbow strike to palm of left hand.

Meaning: double counterattack by defender.

Movement 19a: turn 90° left into a left forward stance facing A and execute a down block with left arm (front view).

Movement 19b: remain in same stance and execute an inner arm block with right arm (front view).

Meaning: double defense: first, against an attack to the lower section, and second, against an attack to the middle section.

Movement 20a: execute a middle section front kick with right foot (front view).

Movement 20b: jump forward (without lowering right foot to floor) into a right twist stance and execute an upper section back-fist strike with right hand (front view). Yell, "Ki hop!"

Meaning: double finishing counterattack by defender.

TAE GEUK FORM SIX

Tae Geuk Yook-Jong

Movement 1: turn 90° left into a left forward stance facing D and execute a down block with left arm.

Meaning: lower section defense.

Movement 2a: execute a middle section front kick with right foot.

Movement 2b: step back with right foot into a left back stance and execute an outer arm block with left arm.

Meaning: counterattack by defender followed by middle section defense.

Movement 3: turn 180° right into a forward stance facing C and execute a down block using right arm.

Meaning: lower section defense.

Movement 4a: execute a middle section front kick with left foot.

Movement 4b: step back with left foot into a right back stance and execute an outer arm block with right arm.

Meaning: counterattack by defender followed by a middle section defense.

Movement 5: turn 90° left into a left forward stance facing B and execute a knife-hand block with right hand.

Meaning: high section defense.

Movement 6: execute a middle section round kick with right foot.

Meaning: counterattack by defender.

Movement 7a: step down with right foot into an open stance for a brief moment facing F, then step forward with left foot into a left front stance and execute an outer arm block with left arm.

Movement 7b: execute a middle section punch with right fist.

Meaning: high section defense followed by a counterattack.

Movement 8a: execute a middle section front kick with right foot.

Movement 8b: step down with right foot into a right forward stance and execute a middle section punch with left fist.

Meaning: double counterattack by defender.

Movement 9a: turn 180° right into a right forward stance facing E and execute an outer arm block with right arm.

Movement 9b: execute a middle section punch with the left hand.

Meaning: high section defense followed by counterattack.

Movement 10a: execute a middle section front kick with left foot.

Movement 10b: step down with left foot into a left forward stance and execute a middle section punch with right fist.

Meaning: double counterattack by defender.

Movement 11a: turn 90° left into an open stance facing B and cross arms before face.

Movement 11b: slowly lower arms before front of body, then execute an open block with both arms.

Meaning: middle section defense against attacks coming from the sides.

Movement 12: step forward with right foot into a right forward stance and execute a knife-hand block with left knife-hand.

Meaning: high section defense.

Movement 13: execute a middle section round kick with left foot. Yell, "Ki hop!"

Meaning: counterattack by defender.

Movement 14: step down with left foot, then pivot right on ball of right foot 270° and step into right forward stance facing H. Execute a down block with right arm.

Meaning: lower section defense.

Movement 15a: execute a middle section front kick with left foot.

Movement 15b: step *back* with left foot into a right back stance and execute an outer arm block with right arm.

Meaning: counterattack and middle section block.

Movement 16: turn 180° left into a left forward stance facing G and execute a downward block with left arm.

Meaning: lower section block.

Movement 17a: execute a middle section front kick with right foot.

Movement 17b: step back with right foot into a left back stance and execute an outer arm block with left arm.

Meaning: counterattack and middle section defense.

Movement 18: turn 90° left and step *back* with right foot into a left back stance facing B and execute a double knife-hand block.

Meaning: middle section defense.

Movement 19: step *back* with left foot into a right back stance and execute a double knife-hand block.

Meaning: middle section defense.

Movement 20a: step *back* with right foot into a left forward stance and execute a palm block with left hand.

Movement 20b: remain in same stance and execute a middle section punch with right fist.

Meaning: middle section defense and counterattack.

Movement 21a: step *back* with left foot into a right forward stance and execute a palm block with right hand.

Movement 21b: remain in same stance and execute a middle section punch with left fist.

Meaning: middle section defense and counterattack.

TAE GEUK FORM SEVEN

Tae Geuk Chil-Jong

Movement 1: turn 90° left into a left tiger stance facing D and execute a palm block with right hand.

Meaning: middle section defense.

Movement 2a: execute a middle section front kick with right foot.

Movement 2b: step back with right foot into left tiger stance and execute an inner arm block with left arm.

Meaning: counterattack and middle section block.

Movement 3: turn 180° right into a right tiger stance facing C and execute a palm block with left hand.

Meaning: middle section block.

Movement 4a: execute a middle section front kick with left foot.

Movement 4b: step back with left foot into a right tiger stance and execute an inner arm block with right arm.

Meaning: counterattack and middle section defense.

Movement 5: turn 90° left into a left back stance facing B and execute a double knife-hand block.

Meaning: low section defense.

Movement 6: step forward into a right back stance and execute a double knife-hand block.

Meaning: low section defense.

Movement 7: turn 90° left into a left tiger stance facing F and execute a palm block with right hand while moving left fist under right elbow.

Meaning: middle section defense.

Movement 8: remain in same stance and execute a high section back-fist strike with right fist.

Meaning: counterattack by defender.

Movement 9: turn 180° right into a right tiger stance facing E and execute a palm block with left hand while moving right fist under left elbow.

Meaning: middle section defense.

Movement 10: execute a high section back-fist strike with left hand.

Meaning: counterattack by defender.

Movement 11: turn 90° left into a closed stance facing B and place palm of right hand over knuckles of right fist and raise fist slowly to chin level at half arm's length in front of body.

Meaning: concentration move—student is preparing himself to explode into action.

Movement 12a: step forward with left foot into a left front stance and execute simultaneous outer arm block with left arm and down block with right arm.

Movement 12b: remain in same stance and execute simultaneous outer arm block with right arm and down block with left arm.

Meaning: double simultaneous defenses for lower and middle sections.

Movement 13a: step forward with right foot into a right forward stance and execute simultaneous outer arm block with right arm and down block with left arm.

Movement 13b: remain in same stance and execute simultaneous outer arm block with left arm and down block with right arm.

Meaning: double simultaneous defenses for lower and middle sections.

Movement 14: turn left 270° into a left forward stance facing G and execute simultaneous outer arm blocks with both arms.

Meaning: middle section defense against double attack.

Movement 15a: execute a middle section strike with right knee.

Movement 15b: jump forward into right twist stance and execute simultaneous middle section uppercut knuckle punches with both hands.

Meaning: double counterattack by defender.

Movement 16: step back with left foot into a right forward stance and execute a low X block.

Meaning: lower section defense.

Movement 17: turn 180° right into a right forward stance facing H and execute simultaneous outer arm blocks with both arms.

Meaning: middle section defenses against double attack.

Movement 18a: execute a middle section strike with left knee.

Movement 18b: jump forward into a left twist stance and execute simultaneous uppercut knuckle punches with both hands.

Movement 19: step back with right foot into a left forward stance and execute a low X block.

Meaning: low section defense.

Movement 20: turn left 90° into a left walking stance facing A and execute a high section side back-fist strike with left hand (front view).

Meaning: defender takes offensive.

Movement 21a: execute inner crescent kick to palm of left hand with right foot (front view).

Movement 21b: step down with right foot into a horse riding stance and execute an elbow strike to left palm with right elbow (front view).

Meaning: double counterattack.

Movement 22: slide right foot back into a right walking stance and execute a high section side back-fist with right hand (front view).

Meaning: defender continues offensive.

Movement 23a: execute an inner crescent kick to palm of right hand with left foot (front view).

Movement 23b: step down with left foot into a horse riding stance and execute an elbow strike to right palm with left elbow (front view).

Meaning: defender continues offensive, forcing opponent back.

Movement 24: execute a knife-hand block with left hand (front view).

Meaning: middle section defenses.

Movement 25: close left hand into fist (grabbing opponent), step forward with right foot into a horse riding stance and execute a middle section punch with right first (front view). Yell, "Ki hop!"

Meaning: grabbing opponent's arm to control him and counterattacking.

TAE GEUK FORM EIGHT

Tae Geuk Pul-Jong

Movement 1a: step forward with left foot into a left back stance facing B and execute an outer arm block with left forearm (palm out) while right arm guards solar plexus.

Meaning: defense against middle section attack.

Movement 1b: slide left foot forward forming a left forward stance and execute a middle section punch with right fist.

Meaning: immediate counterattack by defender.

Movement 2a: leap into the air and execute a jumping front kick with left foot. Yell, "Ki hop!"

Movement 2b: land in a left forward stance and execute an inner arm block with left forearm.

Meaning: defense against an attack to middle section.

Movement 2c: block is followed by two rapid middle section punches, right fist first.

Movement 2d: followed immediately by left.

Meaning: double counterattack by defender.

Movement 3: step forward with right foot into a right forward stance and execute a middle section punch with right fist.

Meaning: continuing attack by defender drives opponent back.

Movement 4: turn left 270°, circling left foot toward G to form a right forward stance while executing an outer arm block with right forearm and simultaneous low block with left forearm. (Note: stance is toward H but defender has head turned toward G.)

Meaning: simultaneous high and low section blocks from opposite directions.

Movement 5: twist body left to change stance into a left forward stance facing G and execute an uppercut punch with right fist while bringing left fist to right shoulder.

Meaning: counterattack against one opponent.

Movement 6: step across right foot with left into a momentary left twist stance facing H, then step out with right foot toward H to form a left forward stance facing G while executing an outer arm block with left forearm and simultaneous low block with right arm. (Note: stance is toward G, but defender has head turned toward H.)

Meaning: simultaneous high and low section blocks from opposite directions.

Movement 7: twist body right forming a right forward stance facing H and execute an uppercut punch with left fist while bringing right fist to left shoulder.

Meaning: counterattack against one opponent.

Movement 8: turn left 90° into a left back stance facing A and execute a knife-hand block with left hand while right knife-hand guards solar plexus.

Meaning: defense against attack to middle section.

Movement 9: slide left foot forward into a left forward stance and execute a middle section punch with right fist.

Meaning: counterattack by defender.

Movement 10a: execute a middle section front kick with right foot.

Meaning: counterattack by defender pushes opponent back.

Movement 10b: bring right foot back to starting position and step back with left foot into a right tiger stance and execute a middle section palm block with right hand.

Meaning: middle section defense.

Movement 11: turn 90° right and step to F with left foot into a left tiger stance and execute a middle section knife-hand block with left hand while right hand guards solar plexus.

Meaning: defense against attack to middle section.

Movement 12a: execute a middle section front kick with left foot.

Movement 12b: step down with left foot into a left forward stance and execute a middle section punch with right fist.

Meaning: double counterattack by defender that drives opponent back.

Movement 13: slide left foot back into a left tiger stance and execute a middle section palm block with left hand.

Meaning: middle section defense.

Movement 14: turn right 180° into a right tiger stance facing E and execute a middle section block with right knife-hand while left knife-hand guards solar plexus.

Meaning: middle section defense.

Movement 15a: execute a front kick with right foot.

Movement 15b: step down with right foot into a right forward stance and execute a middle section punch with left fist.

Meaning: double counterattack by defender that drives opponent back.

Movement 16: slide right foot back into a right tiger stance and execute a middle section palm block with right hand.

Meaning: middle section defense.

Movement 17: turn right 90° into a right tiger stance facing A and execute a right arm down block while left arm guards solar plexus.

Meaning: middle section defense.

Movement 18a: execute a middle section front kick with left foot.

Movement 18b: jump into the air without returning left foot to floor and execute a high section front kick with right foot.

Meaning: combination counterattack by defender that drives opponent back.

Movement 18c: land in a right forward stance and execute an inner arm block with right forearm.

Meaning: middle section defense.

Movement 18d: execute an immediate middle section double punch with left fist.

Movement 18e: followed by the right fist.

Meaning: immediate finishing counterattack by defender.

Movement 19: turn 270° left into a left back stance facing D and execute a middle section knife-hand block with the left hand.

Meaning: middle section defense.

Movement 20: slide left foot forward into a left forward stance and execute a high section elbow strike with right elbow.

Meaning: counterattack by defender.

Movement 21a: execute a high section back-fist strike with right fist.

Movement 21b: execute an immediate middle section punch with left first.

Meaning: double finishing counterattack by defender.

Movement 22: turn 180° right into a right back stance facing C and execute a middle section knife-hand block with right hand

Meaning: middle section defense.

Movement 23: slide right forward into a right forward stance and execute a high section elbow strike with left elbow.

Meaning: counterattack by defender.

Movement 24a: execute a high section back-fist strike with left fist.

Movement 24b: execute an immediate middle section punch with right fist.

Meaning: double finishing counterattack by defender.

4

SPARRING
TECHNIQUES

E very student enjoys the challenge and excitement of sparring. It is
the best way for students to test their practical fighting ability.
Historically, however, the problem with sparring has been to
balance a realistic fighting situation against safety. If students were
allowed to punch and kick at each other without restraint, serious in-
juries would result. To prevent this, different martial art systems have
developed various restrictions on sparring. Some schools allow only
noncontact, or "focus," sparring, in which students score a hit by
delivering a controlled technique to a point approximate one inch from
the opponent's body. This approach has its limits in terms of training for
real-life situations. Students trained this way simply do not understand
what it is like to be hit. Even if such a student effectively blocks or wards
off an attack, the unfamiliar sensation of feeling the force of blows
throws off his concentration and timing. In the worst case, the student
may employ a fancy technique he has developed in the gym only to dis-
cover the hard way that such a technique is ineffective in street combat.

At the other end of the spectrum are those schools that encourage full
contact sparring. The idea of course is to provide as realistic a fighting
situation as possible for the student to develop his or her skills more
effectively. Varying degrees of protective padding are worn by students
to help reduce the risk of injury. Some schools minimize the use of padding to the point of having competitors wearing only boxing-style gloves

and foot pads. This allows the competitors the most freedom of movement but affords little true protection from landed blows. Other schools require their students to don extensive protective gear before sparring including headgear, mouth guard, body padding and leg and arm padding as well as gloves and foot pads. While this in turn affords fairly good protection from even full-strength blows, too much protective gear hampers movement. Moreover, this can make students dependent on the padding to absorb much of the force of a strike, leading to lazy blocking habits. Poor blocking habits can have disastrous results in real-life situations. Without the padded glove to soften the impact of a connecting fist, or the protection of thick body padding to distribute the force of the strike, one punch can do a great deal of damage.

Tae Kwon Do takes a moderate position with respect to sparring rules. While contact sparring is a regular part of training and competition, there are certain restrictions. By requiring competitors to wear protective padding (i.e., headgear, mouth protector, chest protector, forearm and shin pads) and restricting attacks to the front of the body and the head, students are protected from serious injury. At the same time, however, by not encumbering the hands and feet with thick gloves and pads, students are able to block and attack with a great deal of "real-life" force. Furthermore, the protective padding worn in Tae Kwon Do competitions has been specifically designed to be both lightweight and nonrestrictive as well as effective for absorbing the force of landed blows.

Before students are allowed to begin sparring, certain fundamental techniques must be mastered. These techniques allow students to make a smooth transition from the more rigid movements of simple drills to the fluid motions of a competitive fighter. In any sparring situation it is essential that the student be able to move quickly and effectively around the ring. When a student learns to do this properly he is able to manipulate the opponent into revealing momentary openings that may be exploited, and to respond effectively to any movements or changes in stance by the opponent. On the other hand, if a student does not learn to move correctly, chances are good that he'll be an ineffective competitor in the ring. The best techniques in the world will not help him if he cannot get close enough to his opponent to use them, or if he cannot move out of the way of an attack launched by the opponent.

With this in mind, we've devoted the first portion of this chapter to certain drills that will improve your ability to move effectively in sparring situations. These will teach you the basic skills that must be learned in order to become an effective competitor. The first of these drills concerns the basic ways in which to step while maintaining the proper stance and balance. These basic movement drills are the first things to be mastered before a student can hope to become an effective competitor.

BASIC MOVEMENT DRILLS

A   B   C   D

Basic Stepping: The first basic movement is the *forward step*. The illustrations below (A,B,C,D) show a proper forward step. Notice that the master does not change the position of his hands as he steps, nor does he move his eyes away from where the opponent would be. This is the most basic way to close the distance between yourself and an opponent. This is the only time that the feet may be crossed in a sparring situation. It is necessary here to keep the body properly turned at an angle to the opponent.

A   B   C   D

There will be times when either because of the distance between yourself and an opponent or because of the opponent's movement away from you, simply stepping closer will not bring you within sufficient range to strike. In such cases you will need to cover a greater distance. The *skipping step* is a good way to accomplish this. Photos (A,B,C,D) below show how to perform the skipping step. The trick to doing the skipping step properly is to bring the rear foot forward as quickly and as far as possible. Keep in mind that your intention here is to cover a greater distance than with a simple forward step. As its name indicates, the skipping step is used to skip quickly toward your opponent to close the distance between you.

A   B   C

In the preceding examples, the same stance was maintained throughout so that the same side of the body remained leading. An alternate way to close the distance between yourself and an opponent is the *change step*. This movement involves stepping forward and changing the stance from one side to the other. Figures (A,B,C) show this type of movement. Note that the master's hands do not change from left cover to right cover until the final photograph, where his hips and body have turned completely into a right leading stance. This ensures that the body is properly protected. If the hands were to change guard position before the hips were turned, the stance would become awkward and unstable, exposing the student to attack.

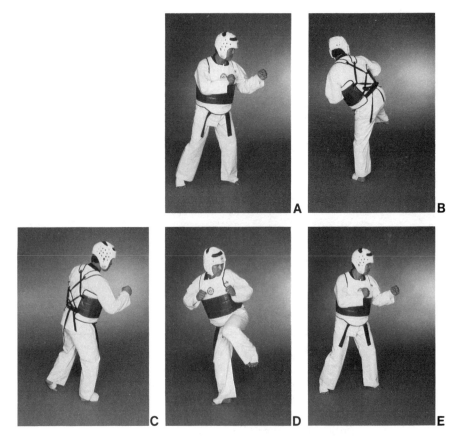

Many kicking techniques in Tae Kwon Do involve spinning the body quickly around to add power. A *spinning step* is a good way to practice this basic motion. Spinning is also a way to confuse the opponent and drive him back. Photos (A,B,C,D,E) show two consecutive spinning steps. If not used as an immediate prelude to a kicking technique, the spinning step can serve not only to close the distance between yourself and the opponent but also to distract him momentarily by giving him the impression that you are about to launch an attack.

A   B   C   D

In all of the preceding illustrations, we have addressed forward and backward motion only. Side stepping, however, is of equal importance. This type of motion is particularly valuable in sparring situations because it allows the student to avoid an attack while remaining within striking range for his own counterattack.

Photos above show a side step to the right (A, B) and a side step to the left (C, D). Note that at the completion of the movement the master is at an angle approximately 45 degrees to the side from that of his starting position. This final positioning takes him away from the direction of the opponent's line of attack and angles him in toward the opponent's side, where the opponent will be momentarily vulnerable to attack. The footwork here is particularly important. The master always uses his rear foot to take the first step. At no time does he allow his feet to cross. This is essential to ensure both the fastest possible movement and the proper position to counterattack the opponent effectively.

SPARRING DRILLS

The preceding set of drills have all dealt with the basic footwork students should know to be able to move effectively in sparring situations. Although each type of motion was presented separately, it is important to remember that often many different movements will be used in combination. It should never be assumed that a single movement will be enough to counter an opponent or set him up for your own attack. Students who have been poorly trained will often make the mistake of moving in a limited and predictable pattern. This is something to be avoided at all costs. Once the opponent has learned to read your intentions, the fight is over. A good fighter must be innovative and unpredictable, moving to no set rhythm or pattern. Such a fighter cannot be read by an opponent and his attacks therefore cannot be anticipated.

Once a student learns to move properly, he must then learn to coordinate those movements with an opponent in a controlled situation.

A countering block or movement is not effective if it is poorly timed. The next set of drills involves the use of a partner. You will notice in the following drills that only a palm block is used when countering the opponent's attack. This is because during actual competition things move far too rapidly for the more formal blocking techniques to be effective. Speed, timing and accuracy are the factors which determine the outcome of a match.

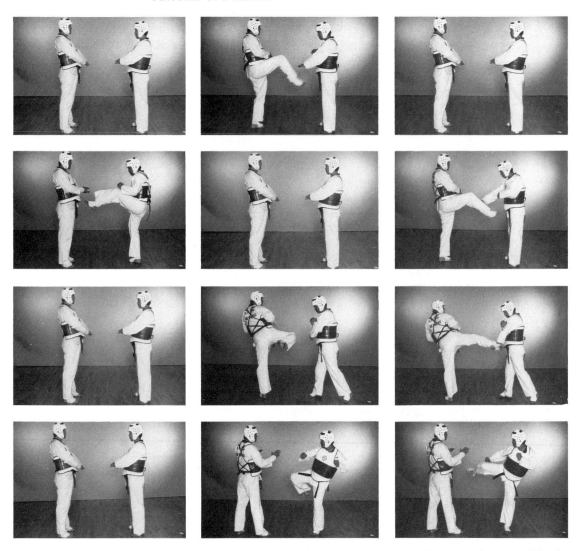

Kick and Block Drill: This first drill teaches students the basics of blocking a kick. Students take turns kicking at each other as illustrated here. One student begins with a kick that the other deflects with a quick palm block. The student who blocked the kick then quickly returns a kick, which the first student then blocks in the same manner. This pattern is repeated as quickly as the students can manage, alternating kicks and blocks with one another to build speed and endurance. Although we have illustrated this drill using only two different kicks, a front kick in the first series and a round kick in the second, any kick can be used.

Kick and Movement Drills: This final series of drills combines what the student has learned from both the basic movement drills and the kick and block drills. Again using a partner, the student performs set counters and defensive movements in response to a predetermined attack. This type of drilling is very important in training instinctive responses to an opponent's attack. For these drills, one student is designated as the attacker and the other as the defender. Timing is controlled by the attacker, who will either hold his position or dance slightly before attacking. In this way the defender's response is spontaneous.

In this first drill, the attacker, on the left, simply steps toward the defender, who steps back out of range. Since no attack was launched by the attacker, there is no need for the defender to do anything else. By stepping away from the opponent, the defender has countered the effect of the attacker's forward step.

Although stepping away from an opponent is an effective way to keep out of range of his attack, it is not a good idea to constantly back away from an opponent. If you constantly back off, you give him the impression that you are afraid of him and he will respond by continuing to advance. Once this is allowed to happen, you put yourself in a position of being overwhelmed by the opponent. One or two steps backward is the most that you should take at any one time.

The second series of illustrations show the attacker, on the right, advancing with a change step. The response in this drill is for the defender to step back and change cover as well. By changing cover, the defender has prevented the opponent from opening up any vulnerable areas to attack.

The third drill shows a combination advance by the attacker, who first uses a change step then moves straight in on the defender. In response the defender first steps back with a change step and then steps directly backward without changing his cover.

In these next drills, the defender not only steps away from the opponent but blocks his attack at the same time. In drill four, the attacker employs a front kick with the back leg. The defender counters this by using a backward change step and blocking the kick.

Drill five shows the opponent using a rear-leg round kick to attack. The response by the defender here again is to step back and change cover while blocking.

The preceding list of drills is by no means exhaustive. Our intention here is merely to illustrate the types of drills that are most effective for training good responses in students who are sparring. Side stepping, combination attacks and attacks involving hand techniques as well as kicks are a few of the other types of drills which train reflexes effectively for sparring. The regular practice of drills of this type will result in the instinctive ability to respond to your opponent's intentions in the ring.

SPARRING TECHNIQUES

The final portion of this chapter deals with actual sparring techniques. Here the masters demonstrate techniques that are effective in actual fighting situations. Bear in mind that the techniques illustrated here are not intended to be learned and memorized step by step. These techniques are presented only to show effective ways of approaching common situations you may encounter in the ring. Often, we have shown more than one means of dealing with the same situation. As we mentioned at the beginning of this chapter, an effective fighter is one who is flexible in his sparring. You will never defeat an opponent with memorized combinations of techniques. Only by remaining alert and adaptable can you succeed in the ring.

None of the photographs in this section have been posed. All pictures presented here were taken during free sparring situations to illustrate the way fighting techniques can be used effectively in real life. To make the following series of illustrations as clear as possible, however, the attacker will occupy the left-hand position unless otherwise stated.

Attack Techniques

One: The attacker begins by skipping in to throw a lead-leg front kick to the middle area followed immediately by a reverse punch to the same area. In this situation the attacker uses speed to surprise his opponent and thereby land his attacks before the opponent can react.

Two: The attacker advances by picking his rear leg up high and stepping in to the opponent as if he were going to deliver a rear-leg front kick. His opponent, however, changes his cover and turns his body to ward off the attack. The attacker uses his forward momentum to step in close to the opponent and deliver a round kick to his middle section right under his elbows. In this situation, the fake kick distracts the opponent from the attacker's real intention, allowing the attacker to score.

Three: In this situation, the attacker first closes the distance by stepping forward, then immediately attacks with a roundhouse kick to the middle section, followed by a reverse punch. Here, the attacker literally charges at the opponent, startling him into momentary immobility, which the attacker takes full advantage of. In this case, however, the opponent had begun to lean away as the kick was thrown. To ensure that he is awarded the point for his attack, the attacker follows up with an unexpected reverse punch.

Four: The attacker closes the distance with a forward step, then launches a side kick to the head, followed by a middle section reverse punch. Here, the attacker purposely draws the opponent's attention to the region of his head with the initial attack. This causes the opponent to pull back and turn away, momentarily leaving his middle exposed, where the attacker scores a hit.

Five: The attacker first closes the distance with a forward skip, then throws a hook kick to the head, followed immediately by a reverse punch to the middle, which scores. This situation is similar to number four, except that the attacker employs a hook kick after closing the distance, which again causes the opponent to dodge the attack to the head and leave his middle section exposed.

Six: Here, the attacker closes the distance by stepping forward and spinning around to deliver a back kick to the middle section. The speed of the back kick makes it a very effective sparring technique, one which is extremely difficult to block. First, the spinning motion disguises the attacker's intention until the kick has actually been launched, giving the opponent no time to react once he has allowed him to close the distance between them. Second, the straight-line motion of the kicking leg allows it to slide in under the opponent's leading arm to score.

Seven: In this situation the attacker employs a spinning hook kick to the head after he has closed the distance with a forward change step. The advantage of a spinning kick is not only in the power that the spin adds to the technique but also in its surprise. In that brief instant that the attacker has spun his back, the kicking leg is hidden and it is extremely difficult to determine what kick will be launched.

Eight: Here, the attacker starts to close the distance by stepping forward, then suddenly leaps in to deliver a roundhouse kick to the head. In this situation the opponent is distracted by what at first appears to be a cautious attempt by the attacker to close the distance between them. The sudden change to a forward leaping-in catches the opponent off guard and does not give him enough time to raise his defenses.

Nine: Here, the attacker attempts to score by using a rear-leg front kick to the middle section. But the opponent is wary of attack and moves away from him with a backward change step. The attacker uses his forward momentum to follow up with an immediate rear-leg roundhouse kick to the middle. (In sparring situations, the opponent is moving around the ring just as much as you are. It would be foolish to expect him to stand still and allow you to hit him.) In this situation, the attacker does not pause after his initial attack fails but uses his own momentum to overwhelm the opponent.

Ten: In this situation the attacker begins with a rear-leg roundhouse kick without attempting to close the distance between himself and the opponent. The opponent avoids the kick by taking a quick step to the rear. The attacker continues his advance by spinning around to deliver a back kick to the middle section. As in situation nine, the opponent avoids the first attack by backing away. Again, rather than pause, the attacker continues to press the opponent with an immediate follow-up technique.

Eleven: As in the preceding situation, the attacker begins with an immediate rear-leg roundhouse kick to the opponent's middle section. Wary of the attack, the opponent moves away with a backward change step at the same moment that the attacker begins to move. Since his initial attack cannot score, the attacker checks his kick and immediately follows up with a second rear-leg roundhouse kick to the head. In this situation the attacker knows not to continue his attack and instead launches an immediate follow-up attack to overwhelm the opponent. By placing his second kick to the head, the attacker catches the opponent by surprise.

Twelve: The attacker begins with an immediate rear-leg roundhouse kick to the middle, which the opponent blocks and slides back from. The attacker then follows up with an immediate spinning hook kick to the head. Here again, as in example eleven, the attacker causes an opening to the head by drawing the opponent's attention to his middle section with the first attack.

Thirteen: The attacker begins by changing his cover, then attacks by skipping forward to deliver a front kick. Here, the change of cover momentarily draws the opponent's attention and causes him to move, making the attack successful. A good rule to remember in the ring is that your opponent is at his most vulnerable when he is moving away from you.

Fourteen: Once again the attacker begins by stepping toward the opponent and changing his cover. Wary of attack, the opponent steps quickly to the rear and changes his own cover. The attacker immediately continues to press his advantage by skipping in to deliver a roundhouse kick. Here again, the value of overwhelming an opponent and keeping him backing away is apparent.

Fifteen: The attacker attempts to score here with an immediate spinning back kick. But the opponent is once again wary of attack and protects himself by stepping to the rear, where he will be out of range. But the attacker sees this over his shoulder as he is about to kick. He checks his back kick and instead leaps in to launch a rear-leg roundhouse kick to the middle section, overwhelming the opponent with the speed of the nonstop combination attack.

Sixteen: Here, the attacker simply takes one step forward and launches into an immediate skipping side kick. Although the opponent attempts to back out of the way, the attacker has gotten close enough with his initial forward step that he can easily overwhelm the opponent with the skipping technique.

Seventeen: In this situation the attacker attempts to score using a rear-leg axe kick. The opponent steps back from the kick to evade it. The attacker continues to press the opponent and as soon as his foot touches the floor he launches a roundhouse kick with the rear leg. This again is an example of drawing the opponent's attention to one area to cause an opening somewhere else.

Eighteen: In this situation the attacker begins with a rear-leg front kick. The opponent, however, steps away from the kick as soon as he sees the attacker begin to move. Since the opponent has stepped out of range, the attacker lunges forward to attack with a rear-leg axe kick. Here, the attacker changes to a different attack that catches his opponent off guard.

Nineteen: In this situation the attacker begins with a quick spinning step to confuse the opponent. He then uses the momentum from the spinning step to throw a jumping roundhouse kick to the head. Here, the added momentum of the initial spinning step helps the attacker launch the jumping round kick with far more speed and power than he could normally.

Twenty: Here, the attacker begins by closing the distance with a forward change step and launching into an immediate jumping roundhouse kick. It is the sudden change of direction that allows the attacker to score.

DEFENSIVE COUNTERATTACK TECHNIQUES

This next series of techniques applies to situations in which the opponent has attacked first. Although it may sound contradictory, your opponent is never as exposed and vulnerable as when he is launching an attack. By extending an arm or a leg away from his body as he attempts to land a punch or kick, he has momentarily opened his guard, giving you the opportunity to counterattack at that instant. Of course, your primary concern will be evading or blocking his attack, but if you learn to do this properly you will also be able to take advantage of the opening your opponent is presenting to you.

In the following examples, the defender will appear on both the right- and left-hand sides, depending on the nature of each technique, to ensure the best camera angle. Just as in the section on attack techniques, all of the pictures presented here were taken during actual sparring situations.

One: The attacker attempts to score here by using a skipping front kick. The defender counters by blocking as he takes a short skip to the rear, then counterattacks with a roundhouse kick to the middle section. The danger of a front kick is that it can slip in under the blocking arm to score. To avoid this, the defender skips slightly to the rear (but only enough to avoid the kick) as he blocks. He is then in a good position to take advantage of the attacker's momentary opening as he retracts his kicking leg.

Because of the frequency with which a skipping front kick attack will be encountered in the ring, the first few examples here will illustrate various ways in which to counter this threat.

Two: Here again, the attacker begins by using a skipping front kick, which the defender again blocks and skips away from. The difference here is that the counterattack by the defender is directed to the head because the opponent is wary of an attack to the body and his guard is strong at his middle section. The decision of where to place a counterattack as well as the type of counterattack to employ is often made in a split second. Only by carefully watching your opponent can you make the right choice.

Three: Once again the attacker leads with a skipping front kick. In this case however, after the defender steps to the rear and blocks, he quickly spins to counter with an immediate back kick to the middle section. Here, the defender makes the maximum use of the attacker's exposed vulnerability during his attack.

Four: In this situation, the defender counters the attacker's skipping front kick by spinning immediately to deliver a spinning hook kick to the head without stepping to the rear. The act of spinning takes the defender out of range of the opponent's attack (because of the forward lean of his body) without his having to step back. The simultaneous counterattack by the defender also catches the opponent at his most vulnerable moment—during his own attack.

Five: As the attacker closes the distance with a skipping roundhouse kick, the defender slides his lead leg back to move himself away from the attack and counters with a spinning hook kick. Here again, the action of throwing a spinning hook kick enables the defender to evade the attacker without stepping to the rear and at the same time catch the opponent at his most vulnerable moment.

Six: Here, the attacker tries to employ immediately a spinning kick in an attempt to score. The defender counters effectively with a push kick. In this situation, the defender does not wait to see what kick the attacker will launch but immediately counters by preventing the attacker from completing his spin.

Seven: As the attacker closes the distance using a change step, followed immediately by a skipping roundhouse kick, the defender skips to the rear to keep himself out of range. As the attacker's roundhouse kick hits empty air, the defender counterattacks with a spinning back kick.

Eight: In this situation the competitors begin by facing each other in opposite leading-side stances. (This is sometimes referred to as an open stance because both competitors are open or vulnerable to real-leg kicks). The attacker ignores this however and leads with a skipping side kick. The defender skips quickly to the rear as he blocks the attack and counters with a rear-leg roundhouse kick to the body, making use of the attacker's exposed position before he can recover his guard.

Nine: In this situation the defender lures the opponent into attacking his middle section by opening his guard. As the attacker skips in to launch a roundhouse kick, the defender immediately spins to deliver a back kick, catching the attacker in motion when he is exposed and vulnerable.

Ten: Here again the competitors are facing each other in opposite lead-side stances, a fact that the attacker again ignores as he leaps in with a skipping hook kick to the head. The defender simply slides his lead leg back and leans away from the kick, then counterattacks with a strong rear-leg roundhouse kick.

Eleven: As the attacker leads with a rear-leg crossing kick from outside to inside, the defender steps to the rear and changes his cover. Then, as the attacker's foot touches down, the defender quickly reverses direction and lands a rear-leg roundhouse kick to the middle section. By stepping to the rear in this situation, the defender brought the attacker and himself back into opposite leading-side stances, from which his rear-leg technique could score.

Twelve: As the attacker attempts to land a skipping roundhouse kick, the defender skips to the rear and launches a roundhouse with the rear leg at the attacker's exposed middle.

Thirteen: As the attacker leaps in to land a skipping roundhouse kick, the defender steps to the side and punches to the middle section. Side stepping is a very effective way to evade an attack while remaining within range to deliver your own counterattack.

Fourteen: When the attacker attempts to land a skipping side kick, the defender steps to the rear and changes cover, moving into an opposite leading-side stance from which his rear-leg roundhouse kick can score.

Fifteen: The attacker leads with a fake front kick using the rear leg, then attempts to score with a front-leg hook kick, since the defender did not step back from the fake kick. The defender in this case simply leans away from the attack. This allows him to counterattack using a rear-leg front kick.

Sixteen: Here, the attacker attempts to land a rear-leg roundhouse kick. The defender blocks the attack as he steps to the rear. The attacker then attempts a second rear-leg roundhouse kick to take advantage of their opposite leading-side stances. Seeing this, the defender sidesteps as he blocks the attack, enabling him to land a punch to the middle section.

Seventeen: As the attacker tries to score with a skipping front kick, the defender skips to the rear and turns quickly to land his own spinning back kick.

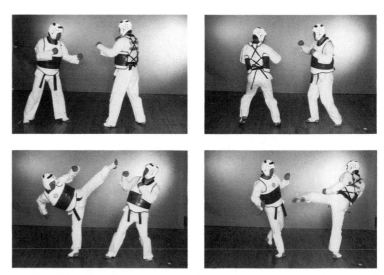

Eighteen: In this situation, the attacker takes a step forward and launches an immediate spinning hook kick to the head. The defender steps to the rear and changes cover, then leans away from the hook kick, in order to land his own counterattacking roundhouse kick.

Nineteen: Here, the attacker drives the defender back with a rear-leg fake kick. As the defender takes a short step backward, the attacker prepares to launch a rear-leg front kick. Seeing his opponent's intention, the defender steps to the rear and changes cover as he prepares to block the kick. The quick response by the defender causes the attacker to hesitate and check his kick. This brief moment of indecision is all the defender needs to counterattack with his own rear-leg roundhouse kick to the middle.

Twenty: Here, the attacker tries a combination attack, first a rear-leg front kick, followed by a rear-leg roundhouse kick. The defender evades the first attack by stepping to the rear and changing his cover as he blocks. Next he steps to the rear and changes his cover again to evade the second attack. Then the defender turns quickly to drive home a spinning back kick as the attacker brings his kicking leg down and tries to consolidate his stance.

5
PRACTICAL
APPLICATIONS

The difference between facing an opponent in the street and facing one in the ring is often no more than a matter of perspective. In the ring, your objective is to score points and evade the opponent's attempts to score against you. In the street your aim is to avoid violent encounters whenever possible. But if this is not possible, your objective is to render the assailant incapable of causing you physical harm. This does not mean, however, that you should attempt to send an obnoxious bully to the hospital simply because he insults your date. The form of the assault dictates your response in a given real-life situation just as the form of attack your opponent employs in the ring dictates your response. In a real-life situation you are not restrained by competition rules and you may have to use the techniques you know in ways that can injure your assailant, but only as a last resort.

The student of Tae Kwon Do gradually develops a sense of inner harmony and discipline that prevents panicking in a dangerous situation. This inner peace comes from the understanding that he is not helpless. His training in Tae Kwon Do has shown him over the years that he is capable of feats of agility and skill that he wouldn't have thought himself capable of before his training. He has learned himself and learned his limits. This spirit should help him to avoid a confrontation. By not allowing the bully to intimidate him, the student is able to avoid a violent confrontation. This is the heart of the teachings of Tae Kwon Do.

However, if your positive spirit is not enough to avoid such a confrontation, beware! If you ever face such a person, you must make certain that he does not have the opportunity to harm you. If you can run away, do so. Standing your ground to display your ability is foolish and dangerous. If he wants your money, give it to him. Money will not help you if he sticks a knife into your body, and he will take your money anyway and leave you lying injured in the street. In short, you should fight only when there is no other option.

If ever you are forced to fight, remember the following guidelines:

1. Assume that your assailant is dangerous—do not underestimate him.
2. Deliver all of your attacks to his most vulnerable points.
3. Never lose sight of your assailant or assume him to be finished after delivering an attack. Remain on guard for him to fight back.
4. After warding off an attack or driving the assailant back, do not stay around. Get away from him as soon as possible.
5. You fight only because you are given no alternative. Do not continue to beat the assailant once he has been rendered helpless.

If forced to fight, these guidelines will help you to remain in control of the situation. Remember that the only way to win a fight is by not allowing yourself to be defeated. If you are able to fight off an assailant and get away without injury, then you have won. It is not necessary for you to do more.

Bearing that in mind, we have illustrated in this chapter a few examples of potential real-life situations and how they may be dealt with. The techniques detailed here are not intended to be memorized the way forms are, but rather to illustrate a number of effective responses to difficult situations.

DEFENDING YOURSELF

A B C D

Here, the master is assaulted by a single attacker who attempts to control him by grabbing his wrist (A). This gives the assailant the advantage of using the strength of both of his arms against a single arm of his victim. The way to counter this kind of grab is to reach *between* the attacker's arms and grab your own hand, as the master does in photo (B). This allows you to use the strength of both of your arms to counter the attacker's two-handed grip. A strong pull away (C) will free your arm. Notice in photo (C) how the master has slipped his left foot behind the attacker's near leg. When he follows up with an elbow strike to the fact in (D), his leg is in place to trip the attacker backward to the ground.

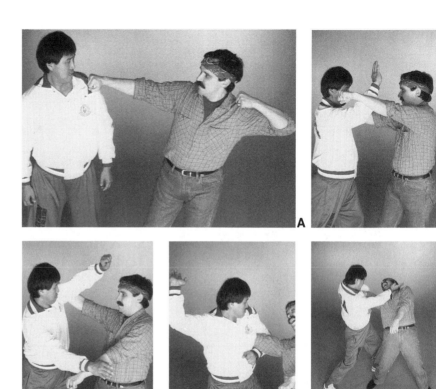

In this scenario, an attacker has grabbed the master by the collar and is about to deliver a punch to the face (A). This is another common form of attack. The immediate concern in this situation is the punching hand. Ignoring the hand holding his collar for the moment, the master brings up his rear hand to ward off the punch using a knife hand block (B). As he sweeps the attacker's hand aside in (C), the master raises his left hand and wraps his arm around the attacker's arm at the elbow (D). By exerting upward pressure with his forearm on the attacker's elbow, the master is able to lock the captured arm straight, causing considerable pain to the attacker in the process. The master is then free to use his right hand to deliver a knife-hand strike to the neck, rendering the attacker unconscious.

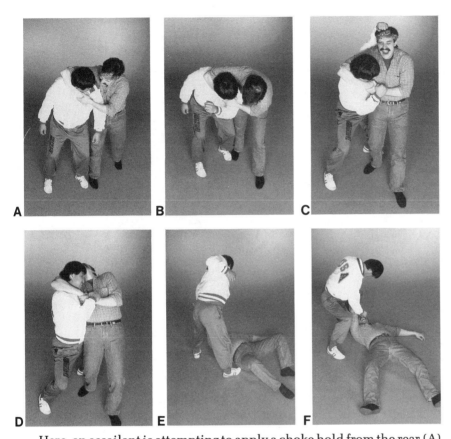

Here, an assailant is attempting to apply a choke hold from the rear (A). This form of attack is extremely dangerous, as it can interrupt the blood flow to your brain and/or crush the trachea (windpipe). To prevent the assailant from gaining a hold, the master immediately turns his head in the direction of the attacker and tucks his chin into his shoulder. By doing this, he protects his throat from injury. Then he leans over and takes a small step forward with his right foot, causing the attacker to bend with him (B). At the same time he brings his left arm forward. Up to this point, the master's responses have all worked to pull the opponent forward and down. The attacker's natural reaction is to control his victim by pulling up and back. This, however, is exactly what the master wants him to do. As soon as he feels the attacker pulling up, the master drives backward with his elbow between the two bodies (a good solid strike to the ribs or solar plexus also produces very satisfactory results) and reaches up across the attacker's back to grab him by the hair (C). Reaching up with his right hand, the master grabs the attacker's left wrist to loosen the pressure on his neck. Notice that as he does this the master also positions his left foot behind the attacker's near leg. By pulling back with his left hand (D), the master easily throws the attacker to the ground (E). From here, a quick punch to the face finishes the attacker (F).

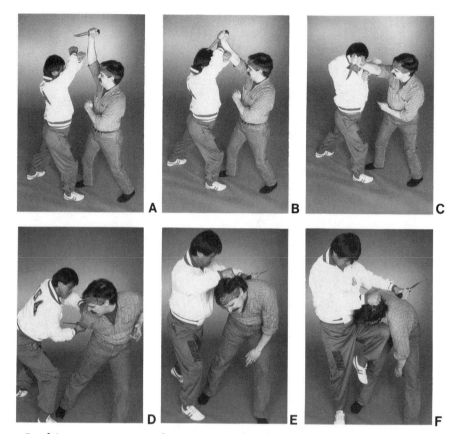

In this next scenario, the master is faced by an attacker wielding a knife. Since he cannot grab the weapon itself without injuring his hands, the only way to neutralize the knife is to control the hand holding it. Accordingly, the master raises both his arms (A) to counter a downward knife strike with an X block (B). At this point, the attacker struggles to force the knife down in an attempt to complete his strike. His own strength can now be turned against him. With the motion of the downward strike stopped and the attacker's knife hand under control, the master grabs the attacker's wrist with his right hand (C) and swings the arm down and across his body (D). While holding the attacker's arm straight, the master then takes the captured wrist with his other hand and forces this arm up behind his back as he grabs the hair on the back of the attacker's head with his right hand (E). He finishes the attacker with a knee strike to the face.

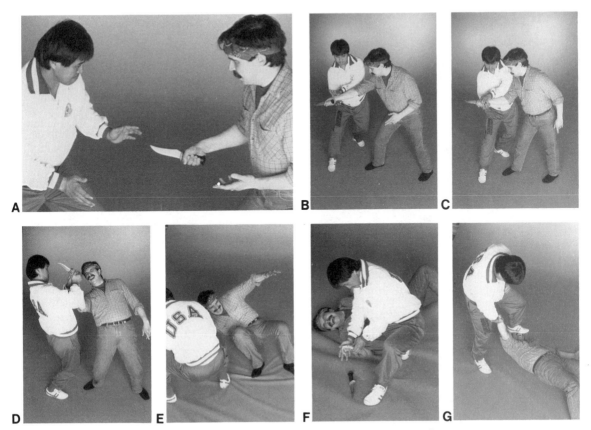

Here again, the master finds himself facing an attacker with a knife. This time, however, the attacker is holding the knife for a lunge strike (A). As the attacker steps forward and stabs, the master quickly steps to the side and deflects the knife hand with his palms (B). Once deflected, the master then grabs the knife hand (C) and twists the attacker's wrist around (D). The master maintains control of the captured wrist and throws the attacker to the ground (E). By continuing to apply pressure to the wrist, the master forces the attacker to drop the knife (F). With the attacker disarmed, the master keeps control of the captured arm as he stands (to keep the opponent from rolling away) and delivers a finishing kick to the face (G).

In this sequence the master uses a variation of the previously illustrated defense against a downward knife strike. The difference here is that the master does not try to stop the motion of the striking arm. Instead of blocking the arm, he redirects it to turn the knife back on the attacker. As the attacker strikes (A), the master steps in and deflects the knife with a right-arm rising block. Notice the angle of the master's arm in this first photo. His forearm is angled in such a way that the opponent's arm does not simply bang against his but is forced to slide down along the outer forearm bone to the right. By grabbing the attacker's wrist (B) he is able to control the knife hand as he pulls it down (C). Using the attacker's own momentum against him, the master redirects the force of the strike and drives the knife into the attacker's groin (D).

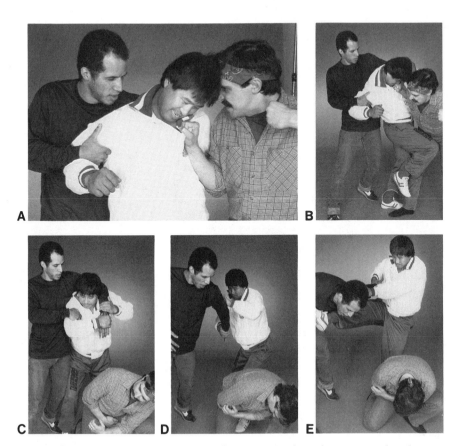

In this next sequence two men have teamed up for an attack. The one in the rear has grabbed both of the master's arms to immobilize him while the other man readies himself to deliver a punch (A). The master realizes that his first priority is the man facing him. Since his arms are tied up, he doesn't waste any time trying to free them. Instead he quickly brings his right knee up into the groin of the first attacker (B). Before the second attacker can react, the master reaches for the hand on his left arm (C). Note that the master takes a firm grasp of the attacker's hand by grabbing it across the back and gripping it tightly along the outer edge. Grabbing the captured hand this way allows the master to control it. The master then ducks under the captured arm (D) and pulls the opponent's arm straight. By applying pressure on the back of the opponent's arm with his left hand, the master is able to lock it straight, so that the opponent is unable to free himself. A finishing kick to the middle is all that is needed to end the confrontation (E).

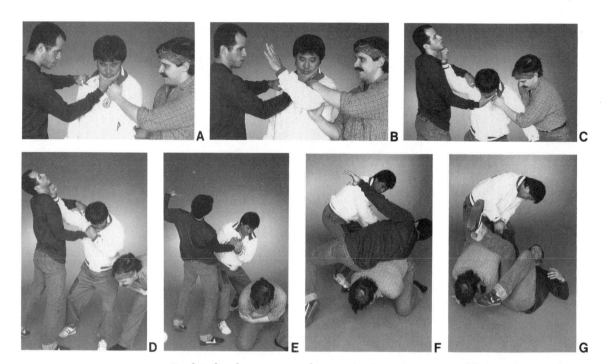

In this final sequence, the master is again accosted by two men. This time, however, they have approached him from both sides (A). Although both attacker's have grabbed him, neither of them has really inhibited his motion. The attacker on the right has grabbed one of the master's arms, but his hold is useless because it is above the elbow. The attacker on the left has grabbed him by the chin, but this is more annoying than effective. The master simply ignores their holds on him and raises his left hand across his body (B). This motion draws the attention of both attackers, momentarily distracting them. The master takes advantage of the distraction by simultaneously delivering a knife-hand strike to the groin of the attacker on the right and an uppercut punch to the chin of the attacker on the left (C). He then peels the attacker's hand from his chin by grabbing the hand firmly at the base of the thumb (D). Taking the captured hand in both of his (E), the master is then able to use that hand to throw the attacker across the body of his accomplice (F) to the ground (G).

6
BREAKING TECHNIQUES

Perhaps the most spectacular aspect of the martial arts occurs when students demonstrate their power by breaking wood and brick with their bare hands and feet. Such feats demonstrate the power and precise control that students can master through the study of our art. Yet aside from promotional tests and public exhibitions, breaking techniques are not a daily part of normal Tae Kwon Do training. The ultimate aim of our art is not to measure our power by the numbers of boards that we are able to smash with our hands, but to improve our bodies and minds. Breaking techniques occupy a secondary consideration in the study of our art in that they serve simply as a means by which we are able to show the level of power that we have developed. This serves students and their instructors as a visible indication of development and control of focus.

Although we have touched upon the concept of focus earlier in the text, we have not discussed the subject in depth. Focus enables students of Tae Kwon Do to develop the ability to break wood and brick. Words cannot express precisely what focus is. Basically, it is the ability to concentrate all of the force of a blow at a specific point in space. This is not the same thing as simple physical strength. A very strong person can smash his fist into a stack of boards but may not be able to break them if he cannot focus his power properly. And even if he is able to break them, it is likely that he will injure himself in the process. Focus is accomplished by allowing the body to relax before the blow is struck. Tension should not enter your body until the moment of impact, at which time all muscles tense. When done properly, a student will be able to concentrate his power in such a way that he not only breaks the target cleanly but also with no pain. As any student of Tae Kwon Do knows from early experience, that very first board probably stung a bit when it broke. This is an example of incomplete focus. Like a spray of water from a hose, the student must learn over the years to concentrate that spray into a single, powerful stream. Later, after he has learned to focus, that board, and indeed an entire stack of boards, will no longer sting his hand.

There is no possible way that focus can be presented in a book, and we will not attempt to do so here. The only way focus can be learned and mastered is through years of practice under the instruction of a qualified teacher. On the following pages, however, we have put together a few examples of typical breaking techniques that students of Tae Kwon Do should be able to accomplish by the time they reach the level of first-degree black belt. Pay attention to the way in which the master concentrates on the target in order to focus the power of his strikes and kicks. Notice also that he holds his hands and feet in a way which enables him to strike with the parts of his body that can most effectively deliver the power of the blow.

Proper Board Holding: Before showing any actual breaking techniques, it is important to illustrate the proper way that boards should be held. The two photographs above show the proper way for holders to position themselves. The boards are first gripped tightly at the corners with the grains all running in the same direction (usually horizontal) and the boards properly aligned. The typical board used for breaking purposes is 3/4-inch pine that measures one foot square. The holders adopt strong front stances with their inner legs leading, and lock their elbows straight. Extra support may be given by having an additional holder or holders stand behind the front holders. In situations where a large number of boards are to be held, they may be either taped together at the top and bottom edges or clamped together with a vise.

It is extremely important for holders to properly support the boards to be broken. Weak support of the boards will allow them to move when struck and the force of the blow will be dissipated. In such a case the blow will simply bounce off, resulting in embarrassment and possibly stinging pain for the student attempting the break. But when held properly rigid, the boards will not move when hit and the student, if done properly, will succeed in driving the strike through them.

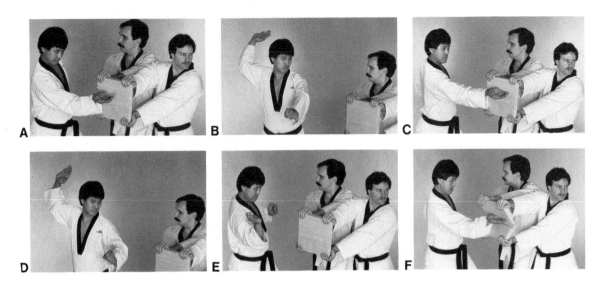

The Knife-Hand: Here, two boards are to be broken using a knife-hand strike. The master begins by assuming a proper stance and locating the center of the target with the striking edge of his hand (A). Next, he takes a practice swing to test his distance (B,C). This is important to assure proper striking angle and distance of the swing and should be done before attempting any breaking technique. When he is prepared, the master raises his arm high behind his head and strikes.

It is important to note in photographs (D,E,F) how the master shifts his weight. In (D) he has brought his weight back over the rear leg as he prepares to strike. In (E) and (F), however, he transfers his weight forward, adding the force of his body's mass to the blow. Such shifting forward of weight is important in generating power properly in any technique.

The Forefist Punch: In this example, two boards are broken using a reverse punch. As with the knife-hand technique, the master begins by assuming a proper stance and locating the center of the target with the striking surface of his hand (A). He next tests his distance with a practice strike (B,C) and then draws his fist back and punches through the target (D,E,F,G). Notice that he adds power to the technique by not only shifting his weight forward but also through the proper use of his hips. By twisting his pelvis quickly, the master is able to move his body to produce a whipping effect that increases the force of his punch.

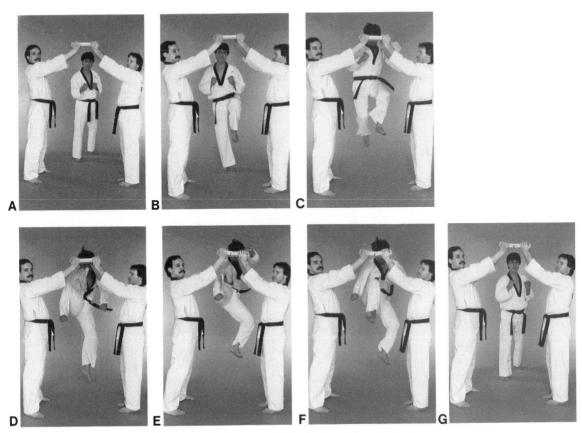

The Jumping Front Kick: Some of the most difficult breaking techniques are done using jumping kicks. Since you cannot get extra help by pushing against the floor with a supporting leg, focus is extremely important in these types of kicks. In this example of breaking, the jumping front kick is used. After testing for distance with a few practice jumps (not shown), the master takes a moment to pause and focus his attention on the target (A). Once he has firmly locked the exact position of the target in his mind, he steps forward and leaps up to deliver the kick. Notice that the kicking foot is the last one to leave the floor. By bringing up the knee of the nonkicking leg first, he gains upward momentum that helps the master lift himself high above the floor. In this example, so precise is the master's control that he is able to break both boards without causing them to fly out of the hands of the holders. This is accomplished only through years of dedicated work and practice. Through concentration and precise control a master of focus can concentrate all of the force of his blow at a specific point in space with dramatic results.

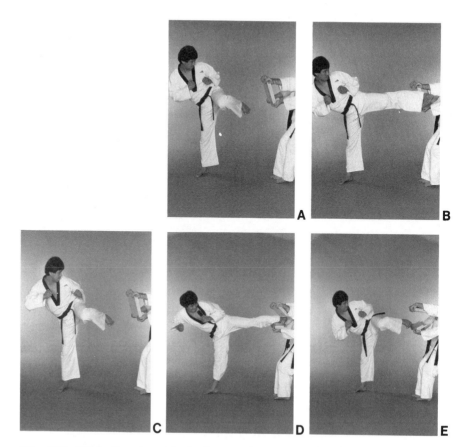

The Side Kick: For the side kick distance is tested by straightening the
leg to the side of the target (A,B). Power is delivered with this kick by
keeping the body leaning as far as possible in the direction of the kick
and shooting the hips into the technique as the leg straightens. This is
one of the most popular and powerful kicks in Tae Kwon Do. The kick
demonstrated here was so quickly executed that even the camera could
not catch it.

The Front Kick: The forward shifting of weight is important to developing power in kicks just as it is in developing power in hand strikes. Notice in this example the look of concentration on the master's face in photograph (F). Such total concentration is what develops focus.

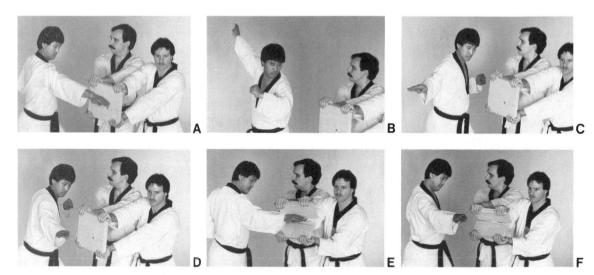

The Ridge-Hand: Again we can see the importance of weight shifting and hip turning in this example, which shows a ridge-hand being used to break two boards. Notice that throughout the entire breaking technique the master keeps his attention focused on the target until he has delivered the strike.

7
THE PHILOSOPHY OF TAE KWON DO

T ae Kwon Do is not just training in kicking, punching and self
defense. It is far more even than training in mental/physical
coordination. A major feature of the art is the development of a
certain *spirit* which carries over into all aspects of life. If there exists a
means through which one could secure a stable, peaceful life, it would
have to be based upon a harmony between oneself and nature. *Do* in
Korean means "art," "path," "way," or "way of life." It is the way in
which the dynamics of the human personality interact with the forces of
the universe. The philosophy of Tae Kwon Do has as its roots many of the
tenets held by religious masters and devout laymen throughout history.
These qualities can be traced back to the influence of Buddhism, and its
aim of the "Mastery Of Self." Buddhism, introduced to the Koguryo
kingdom from China in 347 A.D., contributed greatly to the growth of the
Korean martial arts. The focus of Tae Kwon Do philosophy is to offer a
means by which the student can rid him/herself of the ego, or what Zen-
Buddhists call "discriminating mind," in order to live in harmony with
the universe.

At the core of this philosophy is the concept of 'duality' in nature.
Duality refers to the interaction of opposing forces. Harmony is achieved
when opposite forces are distributed equally, resulting in balance. When
one force dominates however, discord is the result. For example, when
an adversary uses positive (aggressive) energy, or in other words initiates
an attack, the defender should use negative (yielding) energy to respond,
by stepping aside to allow the energy of that attack to flow past harmless-
ly. In this manner, what was once hard (the assailant's attack) becomes
soft (non injurious), and what was soft (the defender's passivity) becomes hard (an effective way to counter a potentially dangerous assault),
allowing balance to return.

Ultimately, the philosophy of Tae Kwon Do seeks to bring students to a level of consciousness known as "Present Time." This occurs when one is completely in tune with himself and nature to the degree that his actions and reactions are always perfectly coordinated with the forces in life whether that be in the sparring ring, in a social setting or even when alone. Such a person cannot be made upset by anything he encounters in life. True masters of Tae Kwon Do are noted for their serene personality which stems from their living in Present Time.

Every person is capable of coordinating him- or herself with the forces in life more perfectly. By centering oneself and balancing the dual forces through living in "Present Time," students can begin to touch the true goal of all human life which is the aspiration to and application of perfection.

RULES OF ETIQUETTE FOR TAE KWON DO PRACTITIONERS

As a community, Tae Kwon Do practitioners have a code of rules which govern interaction among its members. These rules help to maintain the central tenets of Tae Kwon Do: loyalty, respect, courtesy, perseverance and justice.

On the following pages we have compiled a list of these rules of etiquette. You will notice that these rules cover not only the behavior of students while in the school, but also behavior in the outside world. For students of Tae Kwon Do, proper manners are to be practiced continually, not just at the school.

Angle and Posture of Tae Kwon Do: When you bow, you must be in a position of attention with your head bent at 45 degrees and your back at 15 degrees. You must bring the heels of your feet together vigorously.

When Sitting in the School: When a superior sits, you must kneel down and bow.

When a superior enters the school, you must get up from your seat and greet him or her; only after the superior sits down, can you kneel down and bow.

At School: When you enter the school, you must bow to the flag, to the school president, teacher, and to all other higher-ranking black belts.

There should be an absence of unnecessary conversation in the school; students should be dignified and reverent within the school.

The uniform must always be kept with care.

Except on special occasions, you must refrain from wearing your uniform when coming to or going from the school.

Your must use honorific words (sir or mam) when speaking to the president, teacher, or higher-ranking black belts, regardless of their age within the school.

The president, teacher, higher-ranking black belts, or black belts are permitted to speak in non-honorific terms, regardless of age. When not wearing your uniform, you must always respect and obey persons who are five or more years older than you.

Wearing the Uniform and Taking Care of It: The uniform must be kept clean, and you must be neatly dressed.

When your uniform becomes disheveled during practice or a game, you must fix it only after stopping your action and while turned away from all others.

In Society and at Home: You must observe a respectful decorum and speak courteously in home, school, and society.

You must observe the proper decorum, keeping a respectful attitude toward your teachers, superior officers, colleagues, and juniors.

Conversation with Others: Concerning your posture, when you sit and talk with other persons, you must face them with a courteous attitude and an open chest.

The conversation must be executed with a ready smile so as not to give the other person an unpleasant feeling. The conversation must be executed in a low voice, calmly, and in consultation so that the other person can understand.

When having a conversation with another person, you must be careful not to spray saliva.

You must especially be careful about the other person's title or position.

After carefully listening to the other person, you must express your opinion and contention based on true and accurate judgment.

Your must not interrupt another person who is speaking.

You must not stare at another person with a hateful attitude.

When you have a conversation with a superior, you must not touch his body.

Dress and Appearance: Dress must be neat.

You must be formally attired in a tournament, a judgment, or at other events and ceremonies.

Hair must be neatly combed.

You must get used to leading a neat and clean life.

You must not show laziness in your appearance or attire.

Getting in a Car: When getting in a car with a superior, you must always help the superior person into the car first, and when getting out of the car, you must do the opposite, first leaving the car and then helping the superior out.

Telephoning: When you make a telephone call, you should give your name first and then ask about the other person's name.

Eating: You must sit with correct posture when at table.

You must refrain from talking when eating a meal as far as possible.

You must eat only after your superior begins.

Even if the other person is a friend or a guest, you must show him the same respect that you show to a superior.

You must not make unpleasant sounds with your spoon, or while drinking and chewing.

You must eat food with your mouth closed so as not to show the inside of your mouth.

In a Social Setting: When you introduce someone to a superior, you must politely ask the superior's permission, and must introduce his junior to him.

When you have the honor of being introduced, you must wait for the introducing person's word and then greet.

In the event that you shake hands, you must respond only after the superior or the senior person thrusts out his hand.

You must not shake hands too strongly or too limply.

Visiting: Before visiting another person, you must inform that person of your visit, regardless of how high or low his social position is.

If it is possible, you must refrain from visiting on holidays, early in the morning, late at night, meal times, or during bad weather.

If the person is busy or he is not feeling well, you must leave as soon as possible.

Attending to Your Superiors: When entering a room, the attendant must enter first, then stand to one side and allow his superior to enter and lead the way.

Before sitting on a seat, you must wait until your superior is seated comfortably.

During the time that a meeting is in progress, an attendant must always stand guard over the superior, and then must take care in responding to him when necessary.

When the superior expresses his opinion, you must listen carefully.

Seating Arrangements at Ceremonies: The seating must be arranged in the following order: chairman, vice-chairman, director, president, teacher, and higher-ranking black belts. But the chairs should be arranged in such a manner that the center is the top most seat, with the left and right seats flanking the top seat.

When the location of the seating is changed, you must always arrange it in the order of the most superior to the least superior person.

When the chairman and president give a formal address, the seating arrangement is the master of ceremonies first, and then the chairman and president.

When the ceremony ends, the most superior person must get up first followed by the next most superior, etc.

Drinking and Smoking: If and when you receive a cup from a superior, you must take the cup in a restrained manner, and you must drink turning your head away slightly.

You must not spoil any other person's pleasure because of your good or bad feelings.

When smoking in front of a superior, you must refrain from any insulting or disrespectful act (such as blowing smoke in his direction).

Attitude of Leaders (President and Teacher): The president or teacher must have an exemplary personality so that he can be respected by his students.

The president or teacher must be specially careful because the students will follow the example of each and every one of his words and deeds.

Leaders must not slander or defame their companions or superiors in front of their students.

Leaders must refrain from using ugly words or practicing ugly deeds before their students.

The president and teacher must have a definite attitude.

They must not tell lies or use tricks.

They must not talk a lot before their students.

They must carefully consider the family circumstances and difficulties of their students, and must sincerely help them.

They must have a counseling rather than an ordering attitude.

The must correctly distinguish between public and private matters.

The president and teacher must avoid luxury, vanity, excessive merry-making, gambling, excessive drinking, and must show their diligence and frugal life to their students.

The president and teacher must take the initiative in the development of the community and must practice what they preach.

The president and teacher, higher-ranking black belts, black belts, and all Tae Kwon Do practitioners must have an educating and sincere attitude by which they can display a moral spirit, practice justice, righteousness, and humility, and abandon the bad in their life.

APPENDIX A
RULES OF COMPETITION

T he following list of regulations are those currently being used by the World Tae Kwon Do Federation for all official competitions.

Ring Dimensions

For all international championships (including Olympic competitions) the dimensions of the contest area are to measure 26 feet square (8 meters), with the outer boundary measuring 39 feet square (12 meters). The surface of the competition area must be flat and be covered with either WTF approved foam padding or wood.

For all Regional and Local Tournaments the dimensions of the contest area are to measure 19 1/2 feet square (6 meters), with the outer boundary measuring 26 feet square (8 meters).

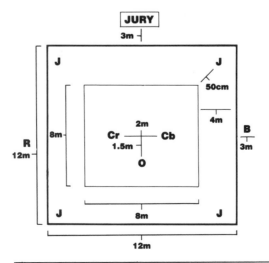

J - Judges' marks
O - Referee's mark
Cr - Red contestant's
      mark
Cb - Blue contestant's
      mark
R - Red coach's mark
B - Blue coach's mark

UNIFORM AND SAFETY EQUIPMENT

Contestants are required to wear the standard white WTF uniform. The uniform must be clean and in good condition, and must be worn in the proper manner (e.g., no colored trim other than black around neck, no rolling up of cuffs or sleeves, etc.).

All contestants are required to wear approved headgear, chest protector, forearm and shin padding (white), and protective cup for men.

All competitors are required to have their nails cut short (both hand and foot), and must securely tie back long hair. Metal objects (jewelry) may not be worn during competition. The restriction on metal objects extends also to eyeglasses (soft contact lenses are recommended for use in competition).

All competitors must keep both themselves and their uniforms clean. Unsatisfactory personal hygiene will result in the automatic disqualification of the violator.

The use of non prescribed drugs or intoxicants by competitors either before or during a match will result in the automatic disqualification of the violator.

A maximum of two layers of tape is permitted except in the case of injury where the tournament physician will approve of its use. No competitor may enter a competition while wearing a splint or cast.

VALID TARGETS

The only targets allowed in competition are on the front of the body between the area of the opponent's waist and the base of the neck (but not the throat itself). No hand techniques may be directed toward the face, although foot techniques are allowed to the head.

OFFICIALS

All competitions are supervised by one referee, four judges, two jurors (one is permitted if a second is unavailable), one time-keeper and one recorder. All officials must be certified by the WTF.

The duties of the referee are as follows:

1. To oversee and control the competition.
2. To inspect all competitors before matches.
3. To provide competition rules, declare the beginning and end of matches, and to give warnings and instructions to competitors.
4. To announce deducted points, disqualifications, signal invalid scores and control all activity within the ring.
5. To oversee the safety of the competitors.
6. To signal stops of the time clock.
7. To collect and submit judges' score cards at the conclusion of each match.
8. To provide opinions to jury requests about judges' decisions.
9. To stop a match (during junior competitions) to consult judges regarding considerations of mismatch and technical knockouts. Such decisions require unanimous agreement by all judges, and jury verification.

The duties of the judges are as follows:

1. To be positioned at each corner of the competition ring and assist the judge as necessary.
2. To advise the referee of invalid violation calls.
3. To note all warnings, points, rule infractions and disqualifications on his score card.
4. To total scores and indicate match winners on his score card.
5. To give completed score cards to the referee following the end of each match.

The duties of the jury are as follows:

1. To consult with judges and referee whenever necessary.
2. To review score cards for consistency, accuracy and signatures of judges, and to bring questions regarding any of the aforementioned to the attention of the judges and/or referee.
3. To determine the winner of a match based on the score cards of the judges and referee.
4. To request the replacement of judges or referees when the performance of these individuals is in question.
5. To sign and submit judges' and referee's score cards to the tournament committee in the event of a protest for the rendering of a final decision.

The duties of the assistants are as follows:

1. The time keeper is responsible for starting and stopping the official clock at the referee's direction, and announcing the end of official time periods.
2. The recorder is responsible for keeping official records of the results of each contest.
3. The weigher is responsible for determining the weight of each competitor according to the regulations of the USTU, in the presence of a designated certified referee.

OFFICIAL LANGUAGE AND SIGNALS

All officials will use the following signals and terminology during competitions:

The Referee

Before Each Match

The referee will call "Cha-ryot" (attention). The palms are lifted to shoulder level facing out with the elbows held in at the sides.

The referee will call "Kyong-ye" (bow). The hands are pushed forward, fingertips pointed, palms facing down with arms parallel to the floor.

The referee will call "Jwa-woo hyung woo" (turn to face each other). The hands are brought back to shoulder level with palms facing each other and wrists straight.

The referee will call "Kyong-ye" (bow). The hands are dropped so the forearms are parallel to the floor with the fingertips almost touching.

The referee will call "Joonbi" (ready). Stepping forward into a left front stance, the right hand is dropped into a knife-hand position, arm straight with the hand directly in front of the solar plexus while left hand is clenched and held straight down at the left side.

The referee will then call "Si-jak" (begin). The left foot is drawn back toward the right as both hands are brought quickly together, palms facing with forearms parallel to the floor.

Time Out

The referee will call "Kyeshi" (time). He will point to the time keeper with the index finger of his right hand to stop the time clock.

The referee will then call "Shi gan" (time out). An ✕ is made with both index fingers by facing both palms out and crossing the fingers at the middle knuckles.

10-Second Count

The referee will position himself 1 meter from the downed competitor and count in one second intervals as the fingers are opened and closed in conjunction with the count.

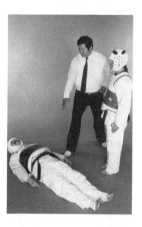

Stopping the Match

The referee will call "Kalyeo" (break). The right hand is dropped in a knife-hand position, with arm held straight out in front of the solar plexus.

Half Point Deductions

After stopping the match, the referee will point to the offending competitor and make one of the following gestures.

Grabbing
The hand is held palm up with the arm extended at a downward angle toward the opponent to be penalized and then brought firmly back toward the shoulder while making a fist.

Pushing
The hands are held palm out and brought back to each side of the chest and forcefully extended, stopping before the elbows reach full extension.

Holding
The arms are slightly rounded with fingertips pointing toward each other as hands are brought back toward the body in a hugging motion.

Crossing the Alert Line
The right hand is dropped vertically in front of the body and then flipped over so the palm faces up.

Turning the Back

The left fist is held at the level of the left shoulder with the palm facing in. The fingertips of the right hand are placed over the back of the left fist.

Intentional Falling

The right elbow is bent at the side of the body with palm facing down and knees bent slightly while the hand is pushed down the side of the body.

Pretending Injury

The fingertips of the right hand are placed over the mouth.

Attacking with the Knee

The right knee is lifted slightly and touched with the fingertips of the right hand.

Attacking the Groin

A point just below the belt is pressed with the fingertips of the right hand.

Kicking the Leg

The right mid-thigh is touched with the fingertips of the right hand.

Hitting the Face

A small circling motion is made with the right fist, which is then brought up to the side of the jaw.

Uttering Undesirable Remarks

The right index finger is brought to the lips.

Full Point Deductions

After stopping the match the referee will raise his index finger above his head and make one of the following gestures.

Attacking a Fallen Opponent

First, a pushing motion is made toward the floor with the appropriate side palm. Next the opposite hand is held open flat at shoulder level with fingertips pointing up while the other fist is brought around to strike the palm.

Attack after Kalyeo (Break)

First, the hands are crossed, palm in, in front of the chest and then separated, palm down, to the outside of the thighs. Next, the opposite hand is held open flat at shoulder level with fingertips pointing up while the other fist is brought around to strike the palm.

Attacking the Back

The fingertips of the hand on the side of the offending contestant is brought to the back of the head. Next the opposite hand is held open flat at shoulder level with fingertips pointing up while the other fist is brought around to strike the palm.

Severely Attacking the Opponent's Face with the Fist

A swift cicular motion is made with the fist to the offending side and then the fist is brought up to the cheek, palm facing out.

Butting

The fingertips of the hand on the offending competitor's side are brought up to touch the forehead while slightly inclining the head forward.

Crossing the Boundary Line

A downward cutting motion to abdomen level is made with the knife-hand on the offending opponent's side, then the hand is turned palm up while the arm is extended to the side.

Throwing the Opponent

The arm on the side of the opponent being penalized is extended straight forward with palm up while the elbow rests on the back of the opposite hand. The extended arm is then flexed toward the same shoulder while clenching the fist. The arm is then swung down until the fist is placed palm down on the opposite arm's elbow.

Violent or Extreme Behavior

The index finger of the hand on the side of the offending competitor is placed over the lips.

To Resume the Match

The referee will use the same signal that was used to begin the competition.

To End the Match

The referee will call "Gu-mahn" (stop). The right hand is dropped in a knife-hand position, with arm held straight out in front of the solar plexus.

To Declare the Winner

Following the end of the match, the referee will collect the score cards of the judges and present them to the jury along with his own completed card. When the jury informs him of the winner, the referee will stand between the competitors facing the jury and grasp their wrists. The referee will then raise the arm of the winner and announce either "Chung sung" (blue wins) or "Hong sung" (red wins).

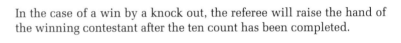

In the case of a win by a knock out, the referee will raise the hand of the winning contestant after the ten count has been completed.

Judges

To Point Out Incorrect Violation Calls
The judge questioning the violation call will rise to his feet in the same spot to attract the referee's attention and announce his contention. If he is not supported in his claim by a minimum of two other judges, he will return to his seat.

Jurors

To Interrupt the Match for Any Purpose
The juror wishing to interrupt the match will say "Chung ji" (stop), then he will inform the referee of the reason for the interruption.

VALID POINTS

The following list of attacks will result in the awarding of one point each for the competitor who executes them with properness of technique, balance and power. The only body areas which may be used to score points are the forefist (fingers must be closed into a fist—open handed techniques are prohibited), and any area of the foot (below the ankle joint). It is important to bear in mind that in order for a punch or kick to be scored as a point, it must land against the opponent's body in an authorized area with sufficient impact force to cause a visible shock to his body.

Foot attack: to any authorized facial or body area.

Hand attack: to any authorized body area (hand attacks are not permitted to the face).

INVALID ATTACKS

A strike to a valid target area will not be awarded a point if the competitor loses balance after completing a valid attack, the competitor is holding the opponent during the attack, or the competitor continues to attack during a clinch.

SAFETY RULES FOR
JUNIOR DIVISION COMPETITIONS

Kicking to the face area must fall within the following guidelines:

a) Complete control of the technique must be demonstrated.
b) Points will be awarded only if the competitor successfully executes the technique with light contact and without causing injury.
c) One point will be deducted if the technique results in a minor injury (an abrasion or bleeding caused by the contact).
d) A competitor will be disqualified if as a result of a kick to the face area the opponent is rendered unable to continue the competition. This determination will be made after a consultation with the tournament physician by the judges, jurors and referee. This determination will not be based on the competitor's inability to continue due to crying, fear, or loss of resolve following a legal attack to the face area.

DEFINITIONS

Knock Down:
a) Whenever any part of the body other than a contestant's feet touch the floor as the result of an attack.
b) Whenever a contestant is caused to stagger as the result of an attack.
c) Whenever a contestant bends over or squats without showing an intention to continue the match.

Knock out:
a) Whenever a contestant cannot continue the match after the referee has completed a count of ten (yol).

Referee stops contest:
a) Whenever the referee or tournament physician determines that the contestant should not continue.
b) Whenever the competitor's coach throws a towel to stop the match.
c) Whenever a competitor protests a referee's call and fails to continue tne match within one minute of the referee's command.

DECISIONS

The winner of a match is determined by a consideration of the following list of criteria:

a) The disqualification of the opponent.
b) The withdrawal of the opponent.
c) The injury of the opponent due to a valid attack.
d) The knock-out of the opponent due to a valid attack.
e) Point difference.
f) The deduction of points during the match.
g) Considerations of superiority.
h) Referee stops contest.

RULES OF SUPERIORITY

In situations where the match results in a tie score, the winner will be decided based on considerations of superiority. The most effective scoring techniques (best single technique) executed by each competitor are compared and rated by the following criteria:

a) A technique of sufficient power to result in an eight-count knock down is considered superior to any other technique.
b) Any foot technique is considered superior to any hand technique.
c) Any jumping kick is considered superior to any standing technique.
d) Any kick to the face is considered superior to any kick to the body.
e) Any counterattack is considered superior to any initiated attack.
f) If the above criteria cannot resolve the tie, the more aggressive fighter is considered superior.

APPENDIX B
THE BELT SYSTEM

A dvancement in Tae Kwon Do is represented by the different colored belts worn by the students. The novice begins with a white belt and advances through progressively darker colored belts until achieving the level of black belt. More than simply indicating a student's rank within the system however, the various belt colors also reflect the central philosophy of Tae Kwon Do. Tae Kwon Do seeks to attune itself with nature, thus the philosophy of the art is based on the cycle of life. Essentially the cycle of life is that living things are born, grow to maturity, leave behind the seeds of new life, then move on to the next plane of existence. Each belt color symbolizes one of the stages in this process.

White	Lack of color, signifying purity and innocence. No knowledge of Tae Kwon Do.
Yellow	The color of the rising Sun, which causes newly sown seeds to germinate and begin to grow. Basic techniques begin to be learned.
Orange	The Sun, deepening in color, rises in the sky, giving its energy to the new growth. Techniques begin to take form.
Green	The color of growing things driving upward. Power begins to be developed.
Blue/Purple	The color of the sky toward which growing things are reaching. Mental and physical power begins to stabilize.
Brown/High Brown	The color of the Earth in which growing things are rooted. Mental and physical power stabilizes.
Red/High Red	The color of blood—the essential force of life. Perfection of character begins to be exhibited by maturity, honor and respect.
Deputy Black/Black	All colors combined. The final stage, where mastery of technique is reflected by calm dignity and sincerity.

WEIGHT AND BELT DIVISIONS

The following divisions are currently being used for all official Tae Kwon Do competitions, including the 2000 Olympics. Unlike the previous regulations, these new divisions do not differentiate between sparring and forms competitions.

Senior Weight Divisions
(Age 17 and Above)

Male:

Fin	not exceeding 54 kg. (118.8 lbs.)
Fly	over 54 kg. not exceeding 58 kg. (118.8–127.6 lbs.)

Bantam	over 58 kg. not exceeding 62 kg. (127.6–136.4 lbs.)
Feather	over 62 kg. not exceeding 67 kg. (136.4–147.4 lbs.)
Light	over 67 kg. not exceeding 72 kg. (147.4–158.4 lbs.)
Welter	over 72 kg. not exceeding 78 kg. (158.4–171.6 lbs.)
Middle	over 78 kg. not exceeding 84 kg. (171.6–184.8 lbs.)
Heavy	over 84 kg. (184.8 lbs.)

Female:

Fin	not exceeding 47 kg. (103.4 lbs.)
Fly	over 47 kg. not exceeding 51 kg. (103.4–112.2 lbs.)
Bantam	over 51 kg. not exceeding 55 kg. (112.2–121.0 lbs.)
Feather	over 55 kg. not exceeding 59 kg. (121.0–129.8 lbs.)
Light	over 59 kg. not exceeding 63 kg. (129.8–138.6 lbs.)
Welter	over 63 kg. not exceeding 67 kg. (138.6–147.4 lbs.)
Middle	over 67 kg. not exceeding 72 kg. (147.4–158.4 lbs.)
Heavy	over 72 kg. (158.4 lbs.)

Junior Divisions
Black Belt: Ages 14–17

Weight	Male	Female
Fin	under 45 kg. (99 lbs.)	under 42 kg. (92.5 lbs.)
Fly	45–48 kg. (99–105.8 lbs.)	42–44 kg. (92.5–97.0 lbs.)
Bantam	48–51 kg. (105.8–112.4 lbs.)	44–46 kg. (97.0–101.4 lbs.)
Feather	51–55 kg. (112.4–121.2 lbs.)	46–49 kg. (101.4–108.0 lbs.)
Light	55–59 kg. (121.2–130.0 lbs.)	49–52 kg. (108.0–114.6 lbs.)
Welter	59–63 kg. (130.0–138.9 lbs.)	52–55 kg. (114.6–121.2 lbs.)
Light-Middle	63–68 kg. (138.9–149.9 lbs.)	55–59 kg. (121.2–130.0 lbs.)
Middle	68–73 kg. (149.9–160.9 lbs.)	59–63 kg. (130.0–138.9 lbs.)
Light-Heavy	73–78 kg. (160.9–172.0 lbs.)	63–68 kg. (138.9–149.9 lbs.)
Heavy	over 78 kg. (172.0 lbs.)	over 68 kg. (149.9 lbs.)

Color Belt: Ages 16–17

Weight	Male	Female
Fin	under 47.7 kg. (105 lbs.)	under 45.4 kg. (100 lbs.)
Fly	47.7–52.2 kg. (105–115 lbs.)	45.4–50.0 kg. (100–110 lbs.)
Bantam	52.2–56.8 kg. (115–125 lbs.)	50.0–54.5 kg. (110–120 lbs.)
Feather	56.8–61.3 kg. (125–135 lbs.)	54.5–59.0 kg. (120–130 lbs.)
Light	61.3–65.9 kg. (135–145 lbs.)	59.0–63.6 kg. (130–140 lbs.)
Welter	65.9–70.4 kg. (145–155 lbs.)	63.6–68.1 kg. (140–150 lbs.)
Middle	70.4–75.0 kg. (155–165 lbs.)	68.1–72.7 kg. (150–160 lbs.)
Heavy	over 75.0 kg. (165 lbs.)	over 72.7 kg. (160 lbs.)

Color Belt: Ages 14–15

Weight	Male	Female
Fin	under 43.0 kg. (95 lbs.)	under 41.8 kg. (92 lbs.)
Fly	43.0–47.7 kg. (95–105 lbs.)	41.8–46.3 kg. (92–102 lbs.)
Bantam	47.7–52.2 kg. (105–115 lbs.)	46.3–50.9 kg. (102–112 lbs.)
Feather	52.2–56.8 kg. (115–125 lbs.)	50.9–55.4 kg. (112–122 lbs.)
Light	56.8–61.3 kg. (125–135 lbs.)	55.4–60.0 kg. (122–132 lbs.)

Welter	61.3–65.9 kg. (135–145 lbs.)	60.0–64.5 kg. (132–142 lbs.)
Middle	65.9–70.4 kg. (145–155 lbs.)	64.5–69.0 kg. (142–152 lbs.)
Heavy	over 70.4 kg. (155 lbs.)	over 69 kg. (152 lbs.)

Color and Black Belt: Ages 12–13

Weight	**Male**	**Female**
Fin	under 38.6 kg. (85 lbs.)	under 37.2 kg. (82 lbs.)
Fly	38.6–43.0 kg. (85–95 lbs.)	37.2–41.8 kg. (82–92 lbs.)
Bantam	43.0–47.7 kg. (95–105 lbs.)	41.8–46.3 kg. (92–102 lbs.)
Feather	47.7–52.2 kg. (105–115 lbs.)	46.3–50.9 kg. (102–112 lbs.)
Light	52.2–56.7 kg. (115–125 lbs.)	50.9–55.3 kg. (112–122 lbs.)
Heavy	over 56.7 kg. (125 lbs.)	over 55.3 kg. (122 lbs.)

Color and Black Belt: Ages 10–11

Weight	**Male**	**Female**
Fin	under 34.0 kg. (75 lbs.)	under 32.7 kg. (72 lbs.)
Fly	34.0–38.6 kg. (75–85 lbs.)	32.7–37.2 kg. (72–82 lbs.)
Bantam	38.6–43.0 kg. (85–95 lbs.)	37.2–41.8 kg. (82–92 lbs.)
Feather	43.0–47.7 kg. (95–105 lbs.)	41.8–46.3 kg. (92–102 lbs.)
Light	47.7–52.2 kg. (105–115 lbs.)	46.3–50.9 kg. (102–112 lbs.)
Heavy	over 52.2 kg. (115 lbs.)	over 50.9 kg. (112 lbs.)

Color and Black Belt: Ages 8–9

Weight	**Male**	**Female**
Fin	under 29.9 kg. (65 lbs.)	under 28.0 kg. (62 lbs.)
Fly	29.5–34.4 kg. (65–75 lbs.)	28.0–32.7 kg. (62–72 lbs.)
Bantam	34.0–38.6 kg. (75–85 lbs.)	32.7–37.2 kg. (72–82 lbs.)
Feather	38.6–43.0 kg. (85–95 lbs.)	37.2–41.8 kg. (82–92 lbs.)
Light	43.0–47.7 kg. (95–105 lbs.)	41.8–46.3 kg. (92–102 lbs.)
Heavy	over 47.7 kg. (105 lbs.)	over 46.3 kg. (102 lbs.)

Color and Black Belt: Ages 6–7

Weight	**Male**	**Female**
Fin	under 25.0 kg. (55 lbs.)	under 23.6 kg. (52 lbs.)
Fly	25.0–27.3 kg. (55–60 lbs.)	23.6–25.9 kg. (52–57 lbs.)
Bantam	27.3–31.8 kg. (60–70 lbs.)	25.9–30.4 kg. (57–67 lbs.)
Feather	31.8–36.3 kg. (70–80 lbs.)	30.4–35.0 kg. (67–77 lbs.)
Light	36.3–40.9 kg. (80–90 lbs.)	35.0–39.5 kg. (77–87 lbs.)
Heavy	over 40.9 kg. (90 lbs.)	over 39.5 kg. (87 lbs.)

APPENDIX C
TAE KWON DO TERMINOLOGY

Anatomy

mo-li: head
eolgul: face
ip: mouth
mok: neck
momtong: body
palkoop: elbow
palmock forearm
sonmock: wrist
son: hand
son-kut: fingertip
joomock: fist
huri: waist
dari: leg
moo-rup: knee
baal: foot
baaldung: instep
dwi-chook: heel
ahp-chook: ball of
  foot

Numbers

Counting

hana: one
dul: two
set: three
net: four
dasot: five
yasot: six
elgub: seven
yodol: eight
ahob: nine
yol: ten

Listing

el: first

e: second
sam: third
sa: fourth
o: fifth
yuk: sixth
chil: seventh
pul: eighth
koo: ninth
sib: tenth

Movements

maggi: block
chi-gi: strike
cha-gi: kick
kyorugi: sparring
jupgi: holding
jirugi: thrusting
twi: jumping
hecho: spreading
modoo: gathering
gong-kyok: offense
hosinsool:
  self-defense

Directions

ahp: front
yop: side
dwi: back
wee: high
gaunde: middle
ahre: low
wen: left
o-ruen: right
dolryo: round
ahn: in (inner)
backat: out (outer)

Stances

cha-ryot sogi:
  attention stance
pyong-hi sogi: ready
  stance
juchoom sogi:
  horseback riding
  stance
ahp-gubi sogi:
  forward stance
dwi-gibi sogi: back
  stance
koa sogi: twisted
  stance
ahp sogi: walking
  stance
bum sogi: tiger stance

Blocks

yeot pero maggi: X
  block
**eolgul maggi (also
  wee maggi):** rising
  block
momtong maggi:
  middle block
ahre maggi: down
  block
son-nal maggi:
  knife-hand block
hecho maggi:
  spreading block

Strikes

chi-gi: forward punch
gullgi chi-gi: hook
  punch

me-joomok chi-gi:
  hammer-fist strike
dung-joomock chi-gi:
  back-fist strike
son-nal chi-gi:
  knife-hand strike
son-nal dung chi-gi:
  spear-fingers strike
pyon-joomock chi-gi:
  knuckle-fist strike
palkoop chi-gi:
  elbow stirke

Kicks

ahp cha-gi: front kick
yop cha-gi: side kick
dolryo cha-gi: round
  kick
dwi cha-gi: back kick
guligi cha-gi: hook
  kick
bandul cha-gi:
  crescent kick
twi o-cha-gi: jumping
  kick

Commands

cha-ryot: attention
  (come to attention)
kyong-ye: bow
joonbi: ready (get
  ready)
dorra: about face
si-jak: begin/start
ba-quo: switch
gu-mahn: hold/stop
barro: return (to
  previous position)

kalyeo: break/stop
kae sok: continue

Titles

kwanjangnim:
master instructor
(above fifth degree
black belt)
sabomnim: instructor
(above fourth
degree black belt)
joo sim: referee

bu sim: judge
bae sim: juror
kae sim: time keeper
ki rohk: recorder

General Terms

poomse: forms
(formal exercises)
kyorugi: sparring
hosinsool: self-
defense

ki-hop: yell (the
power-sound,
which combines
physical and
mental energy)
guk-gi: flag
dobok: uniform
dojang: gymnasium
(for the practice of
Tae Kwon Do)

kwan: school (a
place where Tae
Kwon Do is taught)
jeon: round
(competition
segment)
jeum: point
shi gan: time (time
out)

APPENDIX D
SANCTIONED TAE KWON DO COMPETITIONS

In 1973 the World Taekwondo Federation held the first World Taekwondo Championships in Seoul, Korea. This biannual event is open to all affiliated countries, and competing in the tournament has been the ultimate goal for Tae Kwon Do competitors ever since. As the art has grown in popularity, Tae Kwon Do competition has been included in more and more national and international contests as well. To date, Tae Kwon Do contests are included in the following games:

Pan American Games
Asian Games
African Games
Central American and Caribbean Games
Bolivarian Games
Southeast Asian Games
South American Games
South Pacific Games

APPENDIX E
SANCTIONED NATIONAL
TAE KWON DO ORGANIZATIONS

As Tae Kwon Do has spread throughout the world many organizations have come into being to help promote the art. The following is a list of organizations throughout the world that have been sanctioned by the World Taekwondo Federation. The organizations have been grouped into four regional categories according to geographical location: Africa, Asia, Europe and Pan America.

African Region

Fédération Beninoise de Taekwondo
Federation Burkinabe de Taekwondo
Cameroun Taekwondo Association
Congo Taekwondo Association
Taekwondo Federation of Côte d'Ivoire
The Egyptian Taekwondo Federation
Taekwondo Association of Ethiopia
Association Gabonaise de Taekwondo
Ghana Taekwondo Federation
The Kenya Taekwondo Association
Lesotho Taekwondo Association
The Taekwondo Association of Liberia
Libyan Taekwondo Federation
Association Malienne de Taekwondo
The Malagasy Federation of Taekwondo
Mauritius Taekwondo Association

Fédération Royal Marocaine de Taekwondo
Taekwondo Association of Nigeria
Sierra Leon Taekwondo Association
South African Association for Taekwondo
Sudanse General Association for Taekwondo
Swaziland National Martial Arts Association
Tanzania Taekwondo Association
Fédération Tunisienne de Karaté et des Disciplines Associées
Uganda Taekwondo Association
Fédération Zaïroise de Taekwondo

Asian Region

Afgan Taekwondo Federation
Australian Taekwondo Association
Bahrain Taekwondo Association
Bhutan Taekwondo Federation
Brunei State Taekwondo Association
Chinese Taipei Amateur Taekwondo Association
Fiji Taekwondo Association
Guam Taekwondo Federation

Hong Kong Taekwondo Association
Taekwondo Federation of India
Indonesian Taekwondo Federation
Taekwondo Federation of Islamic Republic of Iran
The Iraqi Taekwondo Federation
Israel Taekwondo Federation
Japan Taekwondo Federation
Jordan Taekwondo Federation
Taekwondo Federation of the Republic of Kazakhstan
Taekwondo Federation of Republic of Kirghizstan
Korean Taekwondo Association
Kuwait Judo and Taekwondo Federation
Lebanese Taekwondo Federation
Macao Taekwondo Association
Malaysia Taekwondo Association
Mongolian Taekwondo Federation
Myanmar Taekwondo Federation
Nepal Taekwondo Association
New Zealand Taekwondo Federation
Ligue de Karaté et Taekkwondo de Nouvelle-Calédonie
Pakistan Taekwondo Federation

Papua New Guinea World
Taekwondo Association
The Philippine Taekwondo
Association
Qatar Taekwondo Association
Samoa Taekwondo Association
Saudi Arabian Karate, Taekwondo
and Judo Federation
Singapore Taekwondo Federation
Solomon Islands Taekwondo
Association
Sri Lanka Taekwondo Association
Syrian Karate and Taekwondo
Federation
Tadzhikistan Taekwondo
Association
Fédération Tahitienne de Karaté,
Taekwondo, Kung-fu et Arts
Martiaux Affinitaires
Thai Taekwondo Association
Tonga Taekwondo Federation
Uzbekistan Taekwondo
Association
Vietnam Taekwondo Association
Yemen Taekwondo Federation

European Region

Federación Andorrana de
Taekwondo
Armenian Taekwondo Federation
Austrian Taekwondo Federation
Taekwondo Federation of the
Republic of Belarus
Taekwondo Federation of Bosnia
and Herzegovina
Union Nationale Belge de
Taekwondo
The British Taekwondo Control
Board
Bulgarian Taekwondo Federation
Croatian Taekwondo Federation
Cyprus Judo, Karate and
Taekwondo Federation
Dansk Taekwondo Forbund
The Finnish Taekwondo
Federation

Fédération Française de Karaté,
Taekwondo et Arts Martiaux
Affinitaires
Deutsche Taekwondo Union
Hellenique Taekwondo Federation
Hungarian WTF Taekwondo
Association
Taekwondo Council of Iceland
Irish Taekwondo Union
Federazione Italiana Taekwondo
Latvian Taekwondo Federation
Lithuanian Taekwondo Federation
Fédération Luxembourgeoise des
Arts Martiaux
Taekwondo Federation of Republic
of Moldova
Taekwondo Bond Nederland
Norway Budo Federation
Polish Sport Taekwondo
Federation
Federaçao Portuguesa de
Taekwondo
Romanian Union of Taekwondo
Clubs
Russian Taekwondo Union
Slovenian Taekwkondo
Association
Federación Española de
Taekwondo
Swedish Budo Federation
Taekwondo Committee
Sektion Taekwondo
Schweizerisher
Taekwondo Federation of Turkey
Ukrainian Taekwondo Federation
Yugoslavia Taekwondo
Federation

Pan American Region

Confederación Argentina de
Taekwondo
Aruba Taekwondo Association
Barbados Taekwondo Association
Bermuda Taekwondo Association
Federación Boliviana de
Taekwondo
Confederaçao Brasileira de
Taekwondo

WTF Taekwondo Association of
Canada
Cayman Islands Taekwondo
Federation
Federación Chilena de Taekwondo
Federación Colombiana de
Taekwondo
Asociación Costarricense de
Taekwondo
Cuban Taekwondo Federation
Federación Dominicana de
Taekwondo
Federación Ecuadoriana de
Taekwondo
Federación Salvadoreña de
Taekwondo
National Taekwondo Federation of
Guatemala
Guyana Taekwondo Association
Taekwondo Union of Haiti
Honduran Taekwondo Federation
Jamaican Taekwondo Association
Federación Mexicana de
Taekwondo
Netherlands Antilles Taekwondo
Association
Asociación Nicaragüense de
Taekwondo
Comisión Panameña de
Taekwondo
Confederación Paraguaya de
Taekwondo
Federación de Taekwondo de
Puerto Rico
Comisión Nacional de Taekwondo
del Perú
St. Vincent and the Grenadines
Taekwondo Association
Suriames Taekwondo Associatie
Republic of Trinidad & Tobago
Taekwondo Association
United States Taekwondo Union
Federación Uruguaya de
Taekwondo
Federacion Venezolana
Taekwondo
The Virgin Islands Taekwondo
Federation

APPENDIX F
MAKING CONTACT

The World Taekwondo Federation

President: Dr. Un-Yong Kim, President
Address: 635 Yuksam-Dong, Kangnam-Ku
Seoul, Korea
Telephone: 82.2.566-2505

Web site: www.wtf.or.kr/home.htm

The United States Taekwondo Union

President: Mr. Sang Chul Lee
Address: One Olympic Plaza, Suite 405
Colorado Springs, CO 80909
Telephone: (719) 578-4632

Web site: www.ustu.com

GLOSSARY

English–Korean

about face: dorra
arm: pol
attention: cha-ryot
attention stance: cha-ryot sogi (or cha-ryot)
back: dwi
back-fist: dung-joomock
back-fist strike: dung-joomock chi-gi
back-hand: son-dung
back kick: dwi cha-gi
back stance: dwi-gubi sogi
ball of foot: ahpchook
begin/go ahead: si-jak
block: maggi
body: momtong
bow: kyong-ye
breathing control: shim ho hyup
break/stop: kalyeo
chest protector: ka soom ho goo
choking-hand: ah-gumson
continue: kae sok
crane stance: haktari sogi
crescent kick: bandul cha-gi
deduction of point: gam jum
down block/low block: ahre maggi
eight: yodul
eighth: pul
elbow: palkoop
elbow strike: palkoop chi-gi
energy (internal energy or life-force): him
face: eolgul
face block/rising block: eolgul maggi (or wee maggi)
fifth: oh
fingertip: son-kut
first: el
fist: joomock
five: dasot
fixed stance (low back stance): go-jong sogi
flag: guk-gi
foot: baal
forearm: palmock

form/pattern/formal exercise: poomse
four: net
fourth: sa
front: ahp
front stance: ahp-gubi sogi
front rising kick: ahp-bodo olligi (or ahp-cha olligi)
front snap kick: ahp cha-gi
front thrust kick: ahp-jillo cha-gi
good-bye: ahn-nyonghi gasipsiyo (to the one who leaves), ahn-nyonghi gesipsiyo (to the one who stays)
go ahead/begin: si-jak
groin defense: noollo maggi
gymnasium (a place for the study of Tae Kwon Do): dojang
hammer-fist: me-joomock
hammer-fist strike: me-joomok chi-gi
hand: son
head: mo-li
healing (through the use of accupressure): googup hwal bop
heel: dwi-chook
Hercules block: kumkang maggi
high: wee
hold/stop: gu-mahn
holding: jupgi
hook, hooking (direction): gullgi
hook kick: gullgi cha-gi
hook stance: koa-sogi
horseback riding stance: juchoom-sogi
how are you?: ahn-nyong hasimnika
in, inner: ahn
inner block: ahn maggi
instep: baaldung
instructor (above fourth degree black belt): sabomnim
judge: bu sim

jury: bae sim
jumping kick: twi o-cha-gi
kick: cha-gi
knee: moo-rup
kneeling: kool o-angi
knife-foot: baalnul
knife-hand: son-nal
knife-hand block: son-nal maggi
knife-hand strike: son-nal chi-gi
knuckle-fist: pyon-joomock
knuckle-fist strike: pyon-joomock chi-gi
left: wen
leg: dari
life-force: him
lotus position (yoga seated posture): baro-angi
low: ahre
low block/down block: ahre maggi
master (above fifth degree black belt): kwanjangnim
martial art/moral culture/way of life: do
meditation: jongsin-tongil
middle: gaunde
middle block: momtong maggi
mouth: ip
neck: mok
nine: ahob
ninth: koo
offense: gong-kyok
one: hana
out, outer: backat
outer block: backat maggi
pattern/form/formal exercise: poomse
point: jeum
pre warning: joo ui
punch: chi-gi
rank: gup (color belt levels other than black belt), dan (black belt levels)
ready: joonbi
ready stance: pyong-sogi (also joonbi)

recorder (tournament official): ki rohk
referee: joo sim
return (to previous or starting position): barro
right: o-ruen
rising block/face block: eolgul maggi (or wee maggi)
rolling/tumbling: goorugi
round (direction): dolryo
round (competition segment): jeon
roundhouse kick: dolryo cha-gi
school (a place where Tae Kwon Do is taught): kwan
second: e
self-defense: hosinsool
seven: ilgub
seventh: chil
side: yop
side rising kick: yop-bodo olligi
side snap kick: yop cha-gi
side thrust kick: yop-jillo cha-gi
six: yasot
sixth: yuk
spar, sparring: kyorugi
spear-hand: sonnal-dung
spear-hand strike: sonnal-dung chi-gi
spreading block: hecho maggi
stance: sogi
stop: gu-mahn
strike/punch: chi-gi
switch: ba-quo
ten: yol
tenth: sib
thank you: gamsa hamnida
three: set
throw, throwing: donzigi
thrust, thrusting: jirugi
third: sam
tiger stance: bum-sogi
time: shi gan

timer (tournament official):
    kae sim
turn around/about face:
    dorra
twisted stance/hook stance:
    koa-sogi

two: dul
uniform (for Tae Kwon Do
    training): dobok
walking stance: ahp sogi
waist: huri
warning: kyong go

way of life/moral
    culture/martial art: do
win: seung
wrist: sonmock
X block: yeot pero maggi

yell (to collect and focus
    internal energy): ki-hop
you are welcome:
    chonmaney

Korean–English

ah-gumson: choking hand
ahn: in, inner
ahn maggi: inner block
ahn-nyonghi gasipsiyo:
    good-bye (to the one who
    leaves)
ahn-nyonghi gesipsiyo:
    good-bye (to the one who
    stays)
ahn-nyong hasimnika: how
    are you?
ahob: nine
ahp: front
ahp-bodo olligi: front-rising
    kick
ahp-cha oligi: front-rising
    kick
ahp cha-gi: front-snap kick
ahpchook: ball of foot
ahp-gubi sogi: front stance
ahp-jillo cha-gi: front-thrust
    kick
ahp sogi: walking stance
ahre: low
ahre maggi: low block/down
baal: foot
baaldung: instep
baalnul: knife-foot
bae sim: jury
backat: out, outer
backat maggi: outer block
bandul cha-gi: crescent kick
ba-quo: switch
baro-angi: lotus position
    (yoga sitting posture)
barro: return (to previous
    position or beginning)
bum-sogi: tiger stance
bu sim: judge
cha-gi: kick
cha-ryot: attention, attention
    stance
cha-ryot sogi: attention stance
chi-gi: punch
chil: seventh
chonmaneyo: you are
    welcome
dan: rank-level/degree (black
    belts only)

dari: leg
dasot: five
do: martial art/moral
    culture/way of life
dobok: uniform used in the
    practice of Tae Kwon Do
dolryo: round (direction)
dolryo cha-gi: roundhouse
    kick
dojang: gymnasium (a place
    where Tae Kwon Do is
    practiced)
donzigi: throw, throwing
dorra: about face/turn around
dul: two
dung-joomock: back-fist
dung-joomock chi-gi:
    back-fist strike
dwi: back
dwi cha-gi: back kick
dwi-chook: heel
dwi-gubi sogi: back stance
e: second
el: first
eolgul: face
eolgul maggi: face
    block/rising block
gam jum: deduction of point
gamsa hamnida: thank you
gaunde: middle
go-jong sogi: fixed stance
    (deep back stance)
gong-kyok: offense
googup hwal bop: healing
    (through to use of
    accupressure)
goorugi: rolling
gullgi: hook
gullgi cha-gi: hook kick
guk-gi: flag
gu-mahn: stop/hold
gup: rank (color belts only
    not including black belt)
haktari-sogi: crane stance
hanna: one
hecho maggi: spreading block
him: energy/internal
    energy/life force
hosinsool: self-defense

huri: waist
ilgub: seven
ip: mouth
jeon: round (competition
    segment)
jeum: point
jirugi: thrust, thrusting
jongsin-tongil: meditation
joomock: fist
joonbi: ready, or ready stance
joo sim: referee
juchoom-sogi: horseback
    riding stance
jupgi: hold, holding
kae sim: timer (tournament
    official)
kae sok: continue
kalyeo: break/stop
ka soom ho goo: chest
    protector
ki-hop: yell to collect and
    focus internal energy
ki rohk: recorder
    (tournament official)
koa-sogi: twisted stance/hook
    stance
koo: ninth
kumkang maggi: Hercules
    block
kwan: school, a place where
    Tae Kwon Do is practiced
kwanjangnim: master (above
    fifth degree black belt)
kyong go: warning
kyong-ye: bow
kyorugi: spar, sparring
maggi: block
me-joomock: hammer-fist,
    side of fist
me-joomock chi-gi:
    hammer-fist strike
mock: arm
mo-li: head
momtong: body
moo-rup: knee
net: four
noollo maggi: groin defense
oh: fifth
o-ruen: right

palkoop: elbow
palkoop chi-gi: elbow strike
palmock: forearm
poomse: form, pattern, formal
    exercise
pul: eighth
pyongi-sogi: ready stance
pyon-joomock: knuckle-fist
pyon-joomock chi-gi:
    knuckle-fist strike
sa: fourth
sabomnim: instructor (above
    fourth degree black belt)
sam: third
set: three
shi gan: time
shim ho hyup: breathing
    control
sib: tenth
si-jak: begin, go ahead
sogi: stance
son: hand
son-dung: back-hand
son-kut: fingertip
sonmock: wrist
son-nal: knife-hand
son-nal chi-gi: knife-hand
    strike
sonnal dung: spear-hand
sonnal dung chi-gi:
    spear-hand strike
son-nal maggi: knife-hand
    block
two-cha-gi: jumping kick
wee: high
wee maggi: rising block, face
    block
yasot: six
yeot pero maggi: X block
yodul: eight
yol: ten
yop: side
yop-bodo olligi: side-rising
    kick
yop cha-gi: side-snap kick
yop-jillo cha-gi: side-thrust
    kick
yuk: sixth

INDEX